The torch is passed···

"...Let the word go forth from this time and place, to friend and foe alike, that the torch has been passed to a new generation of Americans—born in this century, tempered by war, disciplined by a hard and bitter peace, proud of our ancient heritage..."

JOHN F. KENNEDY, INAUGURAL ADDRESS
JANUARY 20, 1961

THE ASSOCIATED PRESS STORY
OF
THE DEATH OF A PRESIDENT

A FOREWORD . . . . . .

One yearns even now, with an almost irresistible force, to be able to file the disclaimer frequently seen at this stage of a book: "All of the characters herein portrayed are fictitious and any resemblance to actual persons, living or dead, is purely coincidental." But the fact won't be wished away and the long night remains, not a bad dream, but a reality to haunt us all the days of our lives.

There is implicit in all human tragedy a waste, a pointlessness. Tragedy unobserved is even more pointless. But tragedy unremembered surely must rank with profound sin. Thus, this chronicle of four days in November, 1963, is written, not to revive shock and tears, but to remember. Thus, we write in the hope that those who come after us will find an insight and a wisdom and a workable moral out of these events which so far elude us who lived them. To those in the future who may learn from the past, this book is hopefully dedicated.

Saul Pett

FRIDAY—November 22, 1963

* * * *

LIKE a great, awkward gull settling onto its nest, Air Force One dropped nose high toward the runway.

The five Air Force officers in their padded cockpit chairs adjusted for a tricky crosswind and the left wheels bit the runway with a screech and puff of smoke. The plane rose, struck the pavement again and stayed, then whined toward the apron where the crowd was waving. Switches off, the engines spun down like dying sirens and the crowd's clamor inherited the air.

It was 11:37 A.M., Dallas time, Friday, November 22, 1963, Love Field.

The door of the cabin opened and the President and First Lady of the United States emerged. They smiled, the sun smiled. They hustled forward to touch fleetingly the writhing arms of the happy throng.

The welcomers were doing their best to give a big Texas "hi y'all" to John Fitzgerald Kennedy and his radiant wife, Jacqueline. Those in back who couldn't quite elbow their way through the milling mob to touch the President's hand or even his dark gray suit held small box cameras overhead hoping to catch something of that famous crinkle-eyed grin. The pros, with their electronic flashguns, scurried backward like burdened crabs for just one more, Mr. President, just one more.

When dawn came that morning, a man was already stirring, up before the womenfolk, getting ready to leave for work. Surely that wasn't his lunch he was wrapping in that brown wrapping paper? The bundle was much too big. The man had surprised everyone by coming home that night to the small house in suburban Irving, just outside of Dallas. Usually on week nights, he stayed in his rented room in town. Maybe he had come out to see his newborn daughter. Or maybe he had come home to get something.

The night before, Mrs. Michael Paine, whose house it was, noticed a light had been burning in the garage. That was where the man kept some odds and ends, including a red-trimmed gray blanket. The man's wife had once seen a rifle wrapped inside and had asked her husband to please get rid of it. He hadn't. Mrs. Paine, a Quaker and a pacifist, would have had a fit if she had known the gun was there. Later that morning, Mrs. Paine would find the blanket empty.

What you got in there? asked 19-year-old Wesley Frazier, a co-worker, as he drove the man to work. Oh, just some curtain rods, said Lee Harvey Oswald.

* * * *

4

It was a big day for Big D. The weatherman had said it would rain but a brisk north wind had blown away the clouds and by mid-morning a warm sun shone. Dallas could congratulate itself. It would get a good look at the President; the bubble top of his limousine would be down.

Dallas is a funny town. It was born out there in frontier country, sure enough, but it hoisted its skirts and tip-toed around the rowdier goings on of the Old West. It was born a business center and business center it remained, population now 750,000 and horizon unlimited. It's a genuinely friendly town yet had become a center of the dark voices who cry the American dream has been turned into a nightmare of sinister treachery: big, choking government, Communist infiltration.

Groups would form, crank out their message on mimeograph, and then disappear from view. A member of the National Indignation Convention said some members wanted to impeach Chief Justice Earl Warren. "I'm for hanging him," he said. The John Birch Society flourished. There was a Dallas Committee to Bring Recognition to Merchants Selling Communist Imports. In the spring someone had painted swastikas on stores owned by Jewish merchants. When United Nations Ambassador Adlai Stevenson had spoken in Dallas October 24, a month before Kennedy's visit, pickets had chanted: "Kennedy will get his reward in hell. Stevenson is going to die. His heart will stop, stop, stop and he will burn, burn, burn."

Later he had been spat upon. After that some Dallas busi-

nessmen had told the Ambassador that Kennedy might be wise to skip Dallas on his upcoming tour. Stevenson told presidential aide Arthur M. Schlesinger, Jr., but nothing came of it.

Not that the Secret Service wasn't busy. After the White House announced the President would visit Dallas, they began the usual preparations. Local police and FBI were asked about known eccentrics. Buildings along the way were checked. Agents would be checking floral arrangements for bombs. The President's steak would be chosen at random from the 2,500 to be served at the luncheon. If someone wanted to poison the President, he would have to poison everybody. There were two possible sites for the President's luncheon speech: the Trade Mart and the Women's Building at Fair Park. The security agents weren't happy about the balconies in the Trade Mart —they could be a roost for a sniper—but on November 16 the Secret Service okayed it for the luncheon. That same day the Dallas Times Herald said the Kennedy cavalcade would probably loop through the downtown area en route from Love Field. The President was bidding for crowds and that's where the crowds would be.

It was logical, a policeman said later, that the motorcade would have to pass the Texas Book Depository Building and this was confirmed November 19 when the official route was published. If the Fair Park had been chosen for the speech, the cavalcade would have passed within sight of the Book Depository Building but much, much farther away. But the Fair

Park wasn't chosen. And Lee Harvey Oswald would have a good chance to see the President, for he worked in the Texas Book Depository Building, a rather wooden name that would dismay writers for years.

* * * *

Somehow there was a rightness to Jack Kennedy that sunny morning at Love Field. He not only was the President, he *looked* it. Young, confident, clean-cut—"vigah" wasn't just a joke, he really exuded it when you saw him in person—a happy, healthy symbol of the might and the invulnerability of his nation. What else was fit to carry him but the noble aircraft behind him with "United States of America" emblazoned along the fuselage? There was in the name and the bold pride with which it was lettered along the big blue and white plane the feeling that nothing could harm its occupant. There was in the man who rode it to so many places around the world a suggested mystique that so many of his friends and aides felt, a feeling that Jack Kennedy always wins, always moves through life in handsome style, never loses.

It might seem unusual that this princely young man, born to riches, raised and educated and wed in an elite world of an Establishment few Americans ever see, should greet with such unfeigned zest the plain, shouting people who crushed around him. But they were the source of his strength. They renewed him and, perhaps, he them.

Yet what really had brought John Kennedy on this mission to Texas was a more prosaic quest—the state's twenty-five electoral votes. He needed Texas in his column in the 1964 presidential race everyone knew he would make. A political feud, however, was threatening to divide the state's Democratic party. It centered around Sen. Ralph Yarborough, a liberal, and Gov. John B. Connally, a conservative. It was complicated by the unspoken position of the Vice President, Lyndon B. Johnson, a Texan himself. It was believed he was in the Connally camp.

John Kennedy came to preserve the peace. He had said at a news conference a few weeks before that Johnson would be his running mate again in 1964. Then, with the unstated gesture typical of him, the President asked Yarborough to fly down with him in the presidential jet to begin the tour.

No one is quite certain when the idea for the trip first took definite form but it was announced September 26, announced as "nonpolitical," which fooled no one. The itinerary was laid out in late October and about a week later the President's wife decided she would go. This was a surprise. The First Lady could smile brilliantly on tour but she really didn't enjoy stumping the countryside. She hadn't done it with her husband since before his nomination in 1960. In fact, her first public appearance since the death of her infant son, Patrick, in August, had occurred Wednesday night just before they left for Texas. She and the President had received the Supreme Court and the federal judiciary in the East Room of the White House.

The preceding week had been about average for the President. Friday he had been in New York where he left police and Secret Service muttering to themselves by spurning a high speed escort and driving into town, stoplight by stoplight, like any other motorist. Guarding the President was difficult enough but what could you do with one who ducked out with a golf cart load of kids to drop in on the corner ice cream store, a President whose wife liked water-skiing off Cape Cod and rode to the hounds in Virginia and on elephants in India? Just as any security agent might have predicted, at Sixth Avenue and 54th Street, the presidential limousine was mobbed by teenagers at a red light. At 72nd and Madison, the car was held up at a light by a nurse who had run out on the street in pursuit of a forgetful patient.

"It's not that we're afraid someone will try to harm him," said a police official, "although that's possible. But we are worried about traffic accidents and the like."

If the President was worried, he didn't show it. He spoke to the AFL-CIO convention in Manhattan and drew a big laugh when he said the man many thought would be his opponent in 1964, Sen. Barry Goldwater, had asked labor's support "before 2,000 cheering Illinois businessmen."

Saturday he was in Florida. "It's fantastic," he said after touring the Cape Canaveral missile base which ten long days hence would bear his name. Sunday was a day of rest at his father's home in Palm Beach. Monday more "nonpolitical" appearances. Tuesday and Wednesday routine desk work back at the White House. Then it was Thursday. Clear the desk. Get ready for the trip. Goodbye to the children, John, Jr.—John-John—who would be three next Monday, and Caroline, who would be six two days later. No need to fret about missing the birthdays. He would be gone only a few days.

* * * *

"All is harmony," Senator Yarborough said, not quite accurately, when Air Force One landed at San Antonio, first stop on the tour. The crowds, if not the politicians, were harmonious. They jammed around the President. "Kennedy in '68" proclaimed a big banner. "Jackie, baby," cried a breezy bystander. There is in American crowds a gay possessiveness about their Presidents. Thus, Truman was "Harry," Eisenhower was "Ike," and the Kennedys were "Jack" and "Jackie." The Kennedys, especially, lent themselves to this easy familiarity. They were young; they were athletic; they were raising a family; their daughter could be seen clomping about in her mother's shoes; their son could be seen crawling under his father's desk; they gave parties; they may have lived on the hill but they shook your hand in a supermarket. A fellow came to feel he almost knew them personally.

The motorcade carried the presidential party from International Airport, San Antonio, to Brooks Air Force Base where Kennedy dedicated a $16 million aero-space medical center. Once again, as he had done many times since the birth of the New Frontier, the President rolled out his familiar cadence and balanced sentence structure to defend the nation's space commitment.

"There will be setbacks and frustrations and disappointments," he said. "There will be pressures for our country to do less and temptations to do something else. But this research must and will go on. The conquest of space must and will go ahead."

John Kennedy always could give a forceful speech even if that New England twang and jabbing finger and staccato delivery didn't meld into the classic picture of an orator. Nor was he a man to turn his back on humor, even at his own expense. The party had gone to Houston that night and the President spoke at a dinner for ailing Rep. Albert Thomas, who had been instrumental in bringing the huge new space

center to Houston, a selection that drew some pointed comments about politics. The President touched off a storm of laughter by congratulating the Congressman for having a part in "firing the largest payroll into space. Er, ah, that's payload, not payroll."

Jacqueline Kennedy, who always seemed to have a knack for just the right little gesture, did it again before the President spoke. They made an unscheduled appearance at a dinner dance of the United Latin American Citizens League and the First Lady gave a short talk—in Spanish. Her dress, a velvet one, was black. After the day was done and the Kennedys had retired to their suite at the Hotel Texas in Fort Worth, Miss Pamela Turnure, Mrs. Kennedy's press secretary, said the First Lady "had enjoyed every moment of it."

Friday was going to be another fast-paced day. There was a breakfast talk in Fort Worth, the luncheon in Dallas and a $100-a-plate dinner that evening in Austin. The Kennedys would spend the night at Vice President Johnson's ranch in Stonewall, 90 miles from Austin.

Apart from the crowds—they were a good augury for '64—and the plug for space, Thursday had been a little irksome. Governor Connally had not invited Senator Yarborough to a reception Friday night. The Senator had twice declined an offer from Vice President Johnson to ride in his limousine during the Thursday cavalcades. And Don Yarborough, no relation to the Senator, who had run against Connally in 1962 on a pro-Kennedy platform, wasn't much in evidence. But the Governor, who had his differences with the President on civil rights and other matters, was riding right up there in the presidential limousine. Well, Friday was another day.

Before breakfast, which was sponsored by the Forth Worth Chamber of Commerce, the President went outside in the mist to say hello to a crowd of people who hadn't been able to get tickets. It was now 8:45. He apologized for his wife not being out yet.

"Mrs. Kennedy is organizing herself. It takes her longer but, of course, she looks better than we do when she does it." It was one of John Kennedy's favorite humor areas. In Paris, he had once introduced himself as "the man who accompanied Jackie Kennedy to Europe."

It was now 9 o'clock. The President had selected for this day a dark bluish-gray two-button suit, gray striped shirt and a dark blue tie figured with lighter blue squares. He wasn't compromising his tailored eastern look in this heart of the cow country. At breakfast he laughed but didn't put on the wide-brim hat presented him. He was always side-stepping the wearing of "funny" hats. He didn't want to be haunted, he frequently said, by any picture like that one of Cal Coolidge wearing an Indian headdress.

"Come to Washington Monday and I'll put it on in the White House for you," he told the breakfast audience.

At breakfast, Mrs. Kennedy got a ringing ovation from the 2,500 guests. She was, as ever, beautiful and stylish, tastefully set out in a strawberry pink suit with a nubby weave and a purplish blue collar. A matching pink pillbox hat perched atop the dark familiar hairdo which had changed the coiffures of a nation.

After breakfast, the leader of the new order paused to pay his respects to the old. President Kennedy called Uvalde, Tex., to wish happy 95th birthday to John Nance Garner, Vice President in the first two terms of Franklin Roosevelt.

It was now 10:35. The presidential party left the hotel for Carswell Air Force Base and the brief hop to Dallas. The base was named in honor of Maj. Horace Carswell, a war hero who was buried in Fort Worth's Rose Hill Cemetery; the same cemetery where a middle-aged woman named Marguerite Oswald had a family plot.

It was now 11:37.

Love Field in Dallas glistened with sunlight on the puddles left by the overnight rain. There was hardly a cloud in the sky as the press plane, the first to land, banked into its approach pattern. Beyond the wing, Dallas looked like a toy city, AP reporter Frank Cormier felt, with gleaming skyscrapers you could almost reach out and touch and rearrange. Air Force Two came in next with the Vice President and his party. The Vice President and President never flew together for security reasons. Lastly, came the big, blue and white "mother ship," Air Force One.

A crowd of several thousand pressed against the fence holding up children kept home from school for the occasion. There were many waving homemade signs of welcome and support. The only discordant note in the sunny mood was a sign held aloft by a man from one of Dallas's silk-stocking neighborhoods. "Help JFK Stamp Out Democracy," it said.

The door of the presidential plane opened and Mrs. Kennedy came out, her pink suit framed in the doorway. Her husband, as ever tugging at his tie and brushing back the clump of hair he never seemed to feel was in place, joined her. They walked down the ramp and up to the greeting committee headed by Dallas Mayor Earle Cabell. Someone gave Jacqueline Kennedy a bouquet of flowers, blood red roses.

"The President was so tanned and healthy, his wife was so lovely, the weather was so perfect, you just felt here was the all-American couple," said a man who was there. The Kennedys had a special sense of identification for young America. She was 34, beautiful wife, young mother, sparkling athlete. He was 46, the war hero who had fought in the ranks with millions of others in World War II, the young skipper of PT 109 who had swum all night pulling an injured shipmate to safety. Now, as President, Kennedy might have Khrushchev on his mind, but he had those two kids to think about, too. Here was the new generation come of age.

At the airport, someone pushed a wheel chair toward the President and he was introduced to Mrs. Annie S. Dunbar, 85. "She's a loyal Democrat and she's never seen a President." Kennedy shook her hand warmly. From the little reception group the President was to have followed his Secret Service escort toward the waiting cars to begin the motorcade. But, instead, he and Jacqueline exchanged quick glances and, like naughty children, stole off toward the fence where the crowd was waving and cheering.

For eight or ten minutes, they walked its length, touching the hands, smiling at the young children held aloft, giving a "hello" or "how are you" to people they had never seen before or would again, people who would never forget that they had seen a President and First Lady. Then, the couple got into the car, and were driven off, leaving behind the bubbling crowd and, out beyond them, the big jet.

It was now 11:52.

The motorcade headed downtown. The streets would be packed during the lunch hour. Earlier that morning handbills bearing a picture of the President had been circulated with the caption: "Wanted for Treason." Also, there had been a full page ad in the Dallas Morning News that day by the "American Fact-Finding Committee" demanding to know, among other things, why the President had "ordered the

Attorney General to go soft on Communism." But these were only tiny ripples, practically invisible in the lake of Dallas's happy mood this day.

In most of the cities the President had toured, crowds stood on the sidewalks barely venturing into the street. Downtown Dallas was different. So many people, friendly people, lined the man-made canyon that they pressed in on the motorcade from left and right. Secret Service agents clambered out of their open touring car—just behind the President's—shooing away an occasional overexuberant spectator.

At Lemmon Avenue and Lomo Alto Street a group of school girls frantically waved a sign: "Mr. President, Please Stop and Shake Our Hands." The President grinned, the convertible halted, the girls giggled, rushed forward and clutched at his outstretched hand. By now, this was the classic picture of John Kennedy, politician. Luckily there was no repeat of the incident in Ireland last summer when the President's car started up and a wellwisher neglected to let go of the Presi-

dent's hand, sending Kennedy and a Secret Service agent sprawling in the back seat. But, as a frustrated agent said after trying to keep up with Kennedy's table hopping at his inaugural ball: "Hell, you can't keep the President of the United States in a steel box."

In Dallas, the big clock on the Mercantile National Bank ticked past 12 noon.

And into the corridor of steel, stone and glass that was the heart of the city rode the motorcade. Shouts and cheers rolled and echoed back and forth mingling with the raucous rumble of the motorcycle escort and their occasional backfires as they jockeyed to keep pace. Newsmen riding in a bus back in the procession thought, all in all, it was a good show for Kennedy.

Prisoners at the towering city courthouse and jail pressed against their bars to catch a glimpse of the President and his wife. It would have been a field day for a thief that noon, for 400 uniformed police were concentrating on the parade route. That was why Officer J. D. Tippit dashed into his home, wolfed

his lunch and dashed out again. With most of the force downtown, he didn't want to stay away too long from the area he patrolled, even though things seemed quiet enough.

The sun glared through the din as the motorcade went down Main Street at 10 or 15 miles an hour. Mrs. Kennedy noted the uproar of the crowds and that persistent sun, but she couldn't take time now to put on sun glasses because she had to wave.

The schedule makers looked anxiously at their watches. It was now almost 12:30, the time the motorcade was due at the Trade Mart. Obviously, things were not running according to plan.

But Mrs. Kennedy's problem with the sun glare would be over in a moment. The motorcade turned off Main Street and had only to make one final turn in front of that big building up ahead. The big building with the long name, the Texas Book Depository Building. Soon the Secret Service would be past this last building it had to worry about. With one more turn, the presidential procession would be on the Stemmons Freeway

riding at flank speed for the Trade Mart.

Up ahead was the promise of shade under a triple underpass. The shouting crowds soon would be left behind. As the limousine neared the book building, Mrs. Connally, sitting in the left jump seat next to her husband, turned around to the President. And to all the irony of the ages, to all the quiet sentences chiselled into the marble of history by subsequent events, Mrs. Nellie Connally of Texas now added her imperishable contribution.

"No one can say Dallas doesn't love and respect you, Mr. President," she said.

"You sure can't," he replied.

The motorcade made the turn and headed for the freeway. The crowd craned for a last look and a waiting eye squinting from above decided it was time.

* * * *

11

The Texas Book Depository Building was certainly nothing to draw the eye that sunny noontime. Someone once had made a try at face-lifting its red brick facade with some white masonry lacework around the entrance. But it remained an unremarkable, doughty fringe resident compared to the shining glass and metal towers the cavalcade had just passed. A building resigned to its fate, cluttered this day, as always, with book cartons, steampipes and cobwebs.

About ninety people worked there. One of them was the man Lee Oswald, a new employe. Manager R. S. Truly had hired him October 15. The salary was $1.25 an hour. He would be working all over the building filling book orders. That was what the building was for. It was a warehouse through which schools all over Texas filled orders for textbooks. A second new man reported for work October 16 and Truly had to decide which one would work at the book building and which at a warehouse, an isolated structure several blocks from the route the President's motorcade would be traveling five weeks later. Truly decided on Oswald for the book building.

Oswald, 24, told Truly he had been a Marine. This was true. He indicated he had been recently discharged. This was not true. There wasn't much more Truly needed to know, just whether the man would do the job. He did. He was industrious. He was efficient. He didn't say much.

That was also the impression of his landlady, Mrs. Arthur C. Johnson. Only she didn't know him as Lee Harvey Oswald. He had taken the $8-a-week room early in October under the name of O. H. Lee, a backward play on his real name. She had asked him for the name of a relative, just in case of an emergency. "Oh, that doesn't matter," he said. Once, a phone call came to the boarding house asking for a Lee Oswald. O. H. Lee was furious.

He rarely went out. He usually got to bed about 9:30. Sometimes he read, sometimes he watched TV—he liked football. Occasionally he would make phone calls but no one knew what he said. He talked in a strange language.

Well, that was his business. Mrs. Johnson was gratified he didn't come in smelling of beer like some of the other sixteen roomers. His room was neat, not that there was much to mess up. A bed, night table, old dresser, wardrobe. Nothing on the chipped, plaster walls. His own radio. A street map of Dallas put out by the Humble Oil people. "When he took a bath he'd clean out that tub as clean as any woman you ever saw," said Mrs. Johnson. On weekends, he'd be gone.

Had Mrs. Johnson been snoopy, she might have learned that O. H. Lee's wallet had a card in it identifying the bearer as A. Hidell. This probably would have puzzled her. It might have given her a start had she known that a Chicago mail order house had sent a rifle March 20 to an A. Hidell in Dallas, a 6.5 mm. Mannlicher-Carcano. And she might have even said "gracious alive!" had she known A. Hidell's box was the same as Lee Harvey Oswald's and Lee Harvey Oswald was O. H. Lee. Or who was who anyway?

The Dallas gunsmith didn't know or care. Nor did the men out at the Sportsdrome rifle range in suburban Grand Prairie. The gunsmith recalled bore-sighting a rifle sometime in October for a man named Oswald. That meant he lined up the telescopic sight on the gun with the barrel. This usually was for a range of 100 yards. All you had to do was line up the cross hairs on the scope on something at 100 yards and squeeze the trigger. The bullet would hit it.

The men at the rifle range knew the face—the almost surly look with a disposition to match. They didn't know the man's name. But the last two weekends before the President's visit they had seen the man do some real shooting. Most of the

men were sighting in their guns for deer season. Garland Slack was getting together some gunners for a turkey shoot.

"I was particularly interested in getting this fellow because he was shooting such a tight group. He could shoot as tight a group as any one there." That meant he could put bullet after bullet into the same spot. Slam down the bolt—bang!—pull it back, slam it forward and down again—bang!—each shot zinging through the hole in the target left by the first.

Gun lovers admire marksmanship like that. Garland Slack never did get that fellow's name, but he was stunned when he recognized him on television a couple of days later.

But being a crack shot didn't pay the rent. So on Friday Lee Oswald was off to work at the book building with a package under his arm. He walked over to the house of Wesley Frazier, a co-worker. Frazier was living with his sister, Mrs. William Randall. Looking out the kitchen window she noticed Oswald had turned up earlier than he usually did. It was now about 7:10 A. M. There was little talk between Frazier and Oswald on the way to work. They got there shortly before 8 o'clock and Oswald went inside with his bundle.

In Fort Worth, it was about the time John Kennedy was getting up to begin his work day. Not that you could compare the two jobs, not with a straight face, anyway. What in the world did the President of the United States have in common with a $50-a-week man who was spending the morning roaming about a building in his dull routine of filling book orders?

That morning five workmen had been laying down plywood flooring on the sixth floor of the book building. About the time John Kennedy was winding up his breakfast talk, one of them, Bonnie Ray Williams, took a break. He sat by the window at the southeast corner chewing on a piece of chicken and sipping soda pop. The crew knocked off for lunch at noon. This was the start of the regular 45-minute lunch break and, besides, everyone wanted to go downstairs when the President was due to pass about 12:25. Everyone but Lee Oswald.

"Let's go down and see the President," said a co-worker to Oswald.

"No. You go on down. And send the elevator back up." The elevator descended. Oswald was alone.

In the musty stillness of the sixth floor, a hand slid open a window. Fresh air wafted in with the murmur of the crowd below. A man moved some cartons over to the window, partially obscuring himself from the outside. Now a new sound drifted in the window. The br-r-r-rum of motorcycles growing louder and louder on a crest of rising cheers. Down at the corner, in front of the county jail, people packed in tighter, jostling for the view down Main Street. The noise quickened and swelled and—there they were! The first of the escort came into sight turning the corner into Houston Street. A noisy serpent, the motorcade, with the motorcycles now in full raucous voice, came on and on and on right toward the building where the man waited. There was the President in full view. Smiling. Waving. Unknowing. Coming...right...down...the...street ...toward...the...window! Now? Now? Now? The motorcade made the sharp left turn in front of the book building onto Elm Street. The first cars. The motorcycles. At last, the President's car. Faster. Faster. Farther. Farther. . . . 50 yards . . . 65 . . . 75 . . . Now? Now? . . . NOW!

"Boy!" said Arnold Rowland, standing below. "You sure can't say the Secret Service isn't on the ball. Look at that guy up there in the window with a rifle."

*   *   *   *

12

A fraction of a second before 12:30 P.M., Friday, November 22, 1963, John Fitzgerald Kennedy was smiling broadly. He would never smile again.

The President probably never heard the shot or knew what hit him. It was a piece of metal a little thinner than an ordinary pencil. It struck him in the back, penetrating two to three inches. He was struck as he turned to his right to wave. His hands snapped up reflexively to his throat. Wordlessly, he slumped over toward his wife, who was sitting on his left in the back seat.

In the jump seat ahead, Gov. John Connally turned and a second bullet caught him in the back, passed through, struck his right wrist and lodged in his thigh. The third and last shot hit the back of the President's head about ear-level, as he was bowed forward.

"His head exploded in blood," said James Chaney, a motorcycle patrolman who was six feet away.

"If I could have, I would have turned away," said AP photographer James "Ike" Altgens, thirty feet away. "Blood covered the whole left side of his head."

Mrs. Kennedy cried out, in the first instant of horror: "Oh, my God, they killed my husband! Jack! Jack!" The verb was already accurate. For all medical purposes, doctors said later, the President was then beyond help. It had all happened in about five seconds.

A motorcycle cop veered toward a curb and almost fell off his machine.... Another officer dropped to the ground, gun drawn.... A man on one of the little greenswards that flanked Elm Street wildly beat his fists on the earth.... A man pushed a woman to the ground protectively....Women ran....Secret Service men behind the President's car pulled rifles and machine guns out of nowhere like lethal magicians.... A man grabbed up his little girl and broke into a run, a policeman in pursuit....Men gasped....What in God's name had happened?...

Altgens, the photographer, fired his camera at the first shot without knowing that he was recording violent history. Suddenly he realized what he had seen through his lens. The thought — the fact — paralyzed him momentarily. Then he snapped again and broke for a phone.

Ten feet away stood Alan Smith, 14, who had skipped school to see the President: "Mr. Kennedy had a big wide smile. When he was hit his face turned blank, no smile, no frown. Nothing. He fell over Jackie's knees and didn't say anything. She stood up screaming 'God, oh God, no!' There was blood all over her and everything. It made me weak. I felt like sitting down." Norman Similas, 34, a Canadian from Willowdale, Ont., in Dallas at a convention, saw a Secret Service man open the car door as the President slumped to the floor. "His head and hair were bathed in blood. The agent looked in and gasped 'My God, he's dead!'"

Mrs. Kennedy, as did many others, thought the first shot was a backfire from one of the many motorcycles. "They can't be firing a 21-gun salute," was the puzzled first thought of the President's Army aide, Maj. Gen. Chester Clifton, who was back in the caravan. But Senator Yarborough felt it was more than that. He had finally accepted Johnson's offer and was riding with the Vice President and his wife, Lady Bird, three cars behind the President.

"It didn't sound like a firecracker," said the Senator. "I knew it wasn't, right off. It was too loud and there was a sort of concussion. I knew right away that something terrible, terrible was wrong."

To Jack Bell, AP reporter in the fourth car, the first shot sounded like a giant firecracker echoing behind him down the canyon of tall buildings. The next two shots exploded those thoughts and Bell lurched for a radio phone.

Dallas Police Chief Jesse Curry, riding at the head of the motorcade, knew disaster had struck. He ordered police to dash back toward that red brick building, the Texas Book Depository Building. Secret Service men in the special car nicknamed the "Queen Mary" had already sniffed trouble like alert bird dogs and had turned back toward the building even while bystanders were still waving joyously at the President.

And there was no doubt in the mind of H. I. Brennan, a

44-year-old steamfitter. He had seen it all. "I saw him. The gun was sticking out the window. I saw him fire a second time. He didn't seem to be in no hurry."

An agent in the President's car grabbed a radiotelephone. "Let's go straight to the nearest hospital!" he shouted to police up ahead. The presidential car, a specially built 1961 Lincoln, broke out of line and screeched off. At speeds reaching 70 miles an hour, rounding some corners on two wheels, it fled toward the hospital, three-and-a-quarter miles distant. Mrs. Kennedy and Mrs. Connally hunched low, cradling their bloody husbands. Agent Clint Hill, who had jumped aboard the car as Mrs. Kennedy reached back to him in a dramatic gesture for succour, shepherded them with another agent who had been riding up front.

"Take it easy!" cried someone. "If he's not dead we don't want to kill him now."

Behind them sped the car of the Vice President who was buried beneath the bulk of Secret Service man Rufus Youngblood. Youngblood, true to the harsh code of his job, had jumped on top of Johnson and his wife, ready to sacrifice his life for theirs.

In the fourth car, the press "pool" car, Bell and Merriman Smith of United Press International were now wrestling for the car's one phone for the biggest story of their lives as the vehicle shot hell-bent up the highway.

Back on Elm Street things were in an uproar. At the first shots someone in the press bus way back in the motorcade cried, "My God, they're shooting at the President!" But no one knew for sure. Some newsmen hollered for the bus to stop. But it sped off to the Trade Mart, dutifully sticking to a schedule that suddenly was no more.

The cameraman, Altgens, dashed to a phone. Bob Johnson, chief of the Dallas AP bureau, took the call.

"Bob, the President has been shot!"

"Ike, how do you know?"

"I saw it. There was blood on his face. Mrs. Kennedy jumped up and grabbed him and cried, 'Oh, no!' The motorcade raced onto the freeway."

"Ike, you saw that?"

"Yes. I was shooting pictures and then I saw it."

Johnson's fingers were already in flight:

BULLETIN

DALLAS, NOV. 22 (AP)—PRESIDENT KENNEDY WAS SHOT TODAY JUST AS HIS MOTORCADE LEFT DOWN-TOWN DALLAS. MRS. KENNEDY JUMPED UP AND GRABBED MR. KENNEDY. SHE CRIED, "OH, NO!" THE MOTORCADE SPED ON.

It sped on, leaving police fanning out looking for something, anything, anywhere. Gun drawn, a motorcycle patrolman ran up to the book building. The manager, Truly, spotted him and dashed into the building with him. Fleetingly, Truly noticed the odd fact that all the elevators were on the top floor. He and the officer ran up the stairs. Puffing behind, Truly reached the second floor to see the officer holding his gun on a man who was sipping a soda pop near two vending machines in a little cafeteria room.

"Does this man belong in here?" barked the policeman.

"Yes," said Truly.

Yes, Lee Oswald worked there.

Satisfied, the manager and the officer left Lee Harvey Oswald at 12:33 and ran off in search of the assassin.

*   *   *   *

In all his years as a priest, Father Oscar L. Huber, 70-year-old pastor of Holy Trinity Church in Dallas, had seen many things, but he never had seen a President. So he walked three blocks from his rectory to the corner of Lemmon and Regan and stood with the nuns and the school children and was thrilled by the historic figures passing before him.

Back at the rectory, he was just finishing up luncheon when the word came that the President had been shot and was being taken to Parkland Hospital. Almost instinctively the old priest hurried upstairs to get his purple stole, ritual book and holy oils for administering the last rites and quickly drove off with Rev. James Thompson, another priest. Parkland was in Father Huber's parish, and he thought he might be needed.

"It just couldn't happen. It just couldn't happen," Father Huber said over and over again as he sped toward the hospital.

At Parkland a young surgeon, Dr. Malcolm Perry, was at lunch in the doctors' cafeteria. The loudspeaker called: "Dr. Tom Shires, STAT. Dr. Tom Shires, STAT." "STAT" meant emergency. Dr. Shires, Perry's superior, was out of town.

"This is Dr. Perry taking Dr. Shires' place."

"The President has been shot," said the operator. "They are bringing him into the emergency room right now."

The press "pool" car had been right on the heels of the racing presidential limousine. Bell jumped out as the cars wheeled and stopped in front of the emergency entrance.

"I saw Mrs. Kennedy, weeping, trying to hold her husband's head up. Mrs. Connally was helping hold up the Governor. Connally's suit front was splattered with blood, his head rolling backward. By the time I had covered the distance to the presidential car, Secret Service men were helping Mrs. Kennedy away. For an instant I stopped and stared into the back seat. Stretched out at full length lay the President, motionless. His natty business suit seemed hardly rumpled, but there was blood on the floor. 'Is he dead?' I asked a Secret Service man. 'I don't know but I don't think so.' The shiny White House automobile, a manufacturer's dream, stood untouched. It had been flown 1,500 miles from Washington only to become the death vehicle of the President it was designed to protect. The plastic bubble top was packed in the trunk. On the front seat lay the soft felt hat the President carried often but seldom wore. Beside it, in mute comradeship, was the wide-brimmed Texas-style hat that Connally wore. Three twisted and torn roses lay in a pool of blood on the floor. Beside them was a tattered bouquet of asters."

Dr. Perry walked quickly toward the emergency section. A nurse pointed to Emergency Room One. The President lay in the small, gray-tiled windowless room on a wheeled aluminum litter. He was stripped to the waist, shoes off, the brace for his bad back still on. Surgeon Charles James Carrico was already at work on him.

Moments before the President arrived at the emergency entrance, a Secret Service agent, face lined with emotion, had dashed in with a submachine gun. Hospital personnel in the emergency room hit the floor for fear the gun would go off. A man in a business suit ran in and the agent slugged him on the jaw before the man, sinking to the floor, could bring out the card that identified him as an agent of the Federal Bureau of Investigation.

Dr. Perry threw his plaid jacket to the floor and a nurse helped him into his surgical gloves. Flash thoughts of what his eyes saw darted through his mind even as his trained hands began to work. "The President, he's bigger than I thought he was." Later: "Here's the most important man in the world." And there was little, so little, that could be done.

Just across the hall in Emergency Room Two doctors were working over Governor Connally. Vice President Johnson had come into the hospital right behind the carts carrying the two men. He was holding his chest.

"Oh, no!" said a reporter. "Not a heart attack." Johnson had had a heart attack in 1955. But this was not another one. There was no clinical cure for the pain he felt this day.

Dr. Carrico had already put a breathing tube down the President's mouth. Dr. Perry inserted another tube through a hole in the throat. By now 15 doctors had assembled. Then they noticed Jacqueline Kennedy standing there, the stains of her husband's blood still on her skirt.

"Would you like to leave, ma'am?" asked Dr. Kemp Clark, a neurosurgeon. "We can make you more comfortable outside."

"No," she said, dry-eyed. But a young medical student saw something else in those eyes. "She was like an animal that had been trapped, like a little rabbit. Brave, but fear was in her eyes."

Outside, there was bedlam. A policeman came out. Reporters swarmed around him. "How is he?" a newsman asked. "He's dead," said the officer. Around the other side of the hospital, in another room, acting White House press secretary Malcolm Kilduff fought off the shouted questions. "I just can't say. I just can't say."

But in Emergency Room One, Dr. Clark knew well enough. Eyes dilated. Fixed. No pulse. All the immutable signs. Still, the doctors worked on.

They hand-pumped Type O negative blood into the President's left arm and leg. A tube was pushed into the chest to keep the lung from collapsing and to suction out blood and air. A machine used to measure heartbeat was attached. A pulsing green band on the scope of the machine would indicate life; a straight line, death. Dr. Clark saw only a straight line.

"It's too late, Mac," he told Dr. Perry. As though he hadn't heard what he heard, Dr. Perry kept on in furious desperation. Kneeling on a stool, he continued to rock his fist rhythmically over the chest of John Kennedy hoping against hope to start the heart back into action. Another machine showed no beat. Three minutes . . . Five minutes . . . Seven . . . Ten . . . Dr. Perry finally gave up . . . No hope. No hope at all. No medical miracle this day. The President of the United States was dead, irrevocably dead. Dr. Perry stepped back helplessly. Dr. M. T. Jenkins turned off the valves of the oxygen system. Dr. Charles Baxter, a surgeon, took a clean sheet and drew it up until it completely covered the President.

Jacqueline Kennedy came forward from the doorway. Dr. Clark led her to the body. She bent and kissed her husband's foot. She took his hand in her own. Father Huber came in for the last rites. Death was no stranger to him. In his long life he had administered the last sacrament hundreds of times and each time he felt the weight of approaching death. But this was different. "It wasn't the blood," he said later. "It was the enormity of it."

Father Huber turned to Mrs. Kennedy.

"I'm sorry. You have my deepest sympathy."

"Thank you," she said.

The sheet was pulled back. Jacqueline Kennedy, married ten years and a widow this day, stood at her husband's right shoulder. She stood tall and erect and unblinking, her face arrested in immobility by a dreadful moment in time, mournful but already gallant in her grief.

Several doctors and presidential aides clustered in the back of the room, trying in the smallness of the place not to intrude on a private moment but halted there by their own shock and tears.

"Si vivis, ego te absolvo a peccatis tuis . . ." Father Huber began the ancient Latin rite of absolution. "If you are living, I absolve you from your sins. In the name of the Father and of the Son and of the Holy Ghost."

He made the sign of the cross on the President's forehead with his thumb, moistened with holy oil.

"Eternal rest, grant unto him, O Lord."

"And let perpetual light shine on him," responded Jacqueline Kennedy. She had taken her husband's right hand as the old priest spoke his words over the first Catholic President of the United States.

Before it was done, Jacqueline Kennedy kissed her husband and took a ring from her finger and placed it on one of his. This was an Irish custom: together in life, together in death. She stood erect again.

"Thank you for taking care of the President," she told Father Huber. "I am shocked," he said, adding, "I am convinced that his soul had not left his body. This was a valid last sacrament."

BULLETIN
DALLAS, NOV. 22 (AP)—TWO PRIESTS STEPPED OUT OF PARKLAND HOSPITAL'S EMERGENCY WARD TODAY AND SAID PRESIDENT KENNEDY DIED OF HIS BULLET WOUNDS.

A mile from Parkland Hospital, a telephone jangled in the front office of Oneal's Funeral Home.

"This is a legitimate call," said an urgent voice. "Load a coffin into your hearse, get a police escort, and get over to Parkland as fast as humanly possible. It's for the President of the United States."

The voice was that of a Secret Service agent. Undertaker Vernon B. Oneal never doubted for a minute that it was a legitimate call.

"What type of casket do you want?"

"The best you have."

It was 1:33 P.M. when Malcolm Kilduff gave the official black word to the clamoring newsmen. He came, red-eyed, into a nurses' classroom where the reporters were gathered. Holding an unlit cigarette, he read from a piece of paper:

"President John F. Kennedy died at approximately 1 P.M. Central Standard Time today here in Dallas. He died of a gunshot wound in the brain."

Many of the reporters there had followed the young President on his campaign trails, on his journeys of state to Vienna and Rome and Paris, on his vacation trips to Palm Beach and Cape Cod. They had written of his gallant candor after the fiasco at the Bay of Pigs, his icy anger in the storm over the steel price increase, his cool resolution as the world edged toward nuclear war in the Cuban crisis. They had written of the man and his grace and his style and his elegant wit, of his wife and his children. Many had become his friends through the short, crowded years. And now they were racing to the phones, hearts heavy, legs pumping instinctively.

FLASH
DALLAS (AP)—PRESIDENT KENNEDY DIED AT 1 P.M. (CST).

Later, Dr. Malcolm Perry sat at home as his children skipped around him lobbying for attention. "I'm tired," he said to his wife. "I've never been so tired in my life."

* * * *

THE MOMENT OF ASSASSINATION

AP Photographer James Altgens took this historic photograph just seconds after an assassin fired the shots that killed President Kennedy. The President's left arm has just jerked up convulsively. Mrs. Kennedy's gloved hand reaches out in support. Behind the tree stands the white facade of The Texas Book Depository Building where the shots were fired from a sixth floor window. The Lyndon Johnsons are riding in the third car. Opposite page, *Top*: A second Altgens photograph shows Secret Service Agent Clint Hill leaping toward Mrs. Kennedy as she desperately moves for help in the first moment of horror. *Middle*: With the President slumped down on the seat and his foot protruding over the side, the presidential car races for Parkland Hospital. *Bottom*: With machine guns out and ready, Secret Service men speed behind presidential car, both vehicles now moving at 70 miles an hour.

At the Trade Mart the word came that the President wasn't coming—would never come.

The organist had been warming up with several choruses of "Hail to the Chief." Several of the guests already were cutting into their steaks. Then a man came to the rostrum and said in a halting voice that the President had been shot. People wept and turned, dazed, to complete strangers. Waiters, nothing to do now, mopped their eyes with napkins. The fountains, which always splashed pleasantly in the huge building, were turned off. The twittering of the many parakeets caged in the balconies of the hall could be heard in the silence.

And in an upstairs room, there was the red phone that was always within the President's reach to link him instantly with the nation's striking force. Nearby stood a straight-backed rocker, empty.

* * * *

AND THE word went out from that time and place and cut the heart of a nation. In streets and offices and homes and stores, in lunch rooms and show rooms and school rooms and board rooms, on highways and prairies and beaches and mountain tops, in endless places crowded and sparse, near and far, white and black, Republican and Democrat, management and labor, the word went out and cut the heart of a nation. And husbands called wives and wives called friends and teachers told students and motorists stopped to listen on car radios and stranger told stranger. Oh, no! we cried from hearts stopped by shock, from minds fighting the word, but the word came roaring back, true, true, true, and disbelief dissolved in tears, more tears probably than this nation has shed over any single event in history. Incredibly, in a time of great numbers, in a time of repeated reminders that millions would die in a nuclear war, in a time when experts feared we were being numbed by numbers and immunized against tragedy, the death of a single man crowded into our souls and flooded our hearts and filled all the paths of our lives.

* * * *

WASHINGTON reeled. Stunned and incredulous, people poured out of government office buildings and department stores, barber shops and supermarkets. A small crowd gathered outside the White House gates, drawn to the consoling security of its pillared elegance. Around the city, little knots of people stood in shocked silence listening to transistor radios. In the unseasonably warm sunshine, a sense of loss, a sense of fury and frustration fell on the lovely old town like a chilling fog, saturating the air with gloom and sorrow, penetrating every tavern corner where a TV set hung, every office cubicle where phones jangled out the horror. Taxi drivers rolled down their windows to shout the news to passersby. The late lunch crowd heard

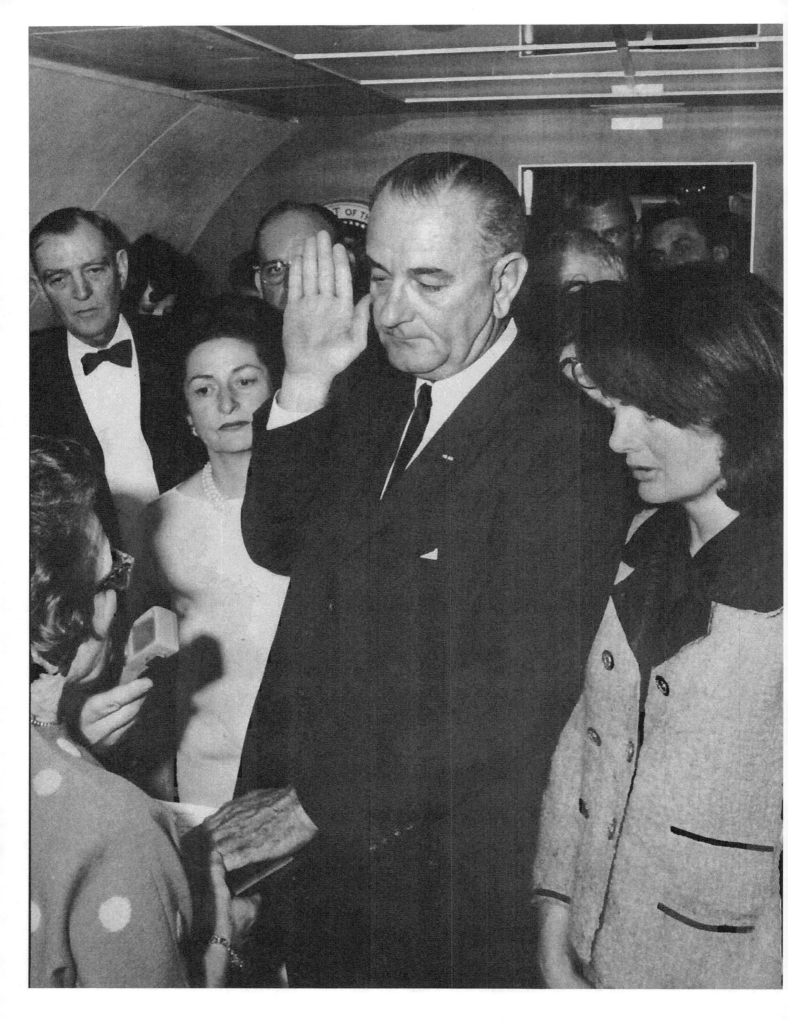

it in the astonished whispers of busboys and waiters. Switchboards were swamped all over town. Women wept openly in the streets and men choked back sobs. Churches suddenly began to fill up at a time of day when the janitor is normally alone with his chores. Then, in the void of further detail, human nature tumbled a bit. Rumors raced through the streets ...Johnson was dead, too...He was shot...No, he had clutched his side and suffered a heart attack...Joseph Kennedy, hearing the news in Hyannis Port, had had another stroke and died...

For others, there was little time for tears or wild fears.

The flash broke up a budget meeting in the Pentagon led by Defense Secretary Robert McNamara. Presidential aide McGeorge Bundy, Budget Director Kermit Gordon, Deputy Defense Secretary Roswell Gilpatric and others fanned out to their offices, while McNamara stuck by the communications complex linking him with armed forces all over the world.

The Joint Chiefs of Staff had scheduled a 2 o'clock meeting with some West German military leaders, but at the first word of the gunshots in Dallas they hurried into session. While they had the standby powers to step up the nation's defense posture from DEFCON Five (normal peacetime) to DEFCON One (all out war alert), they weighed the crisis and settled on a less dramatic course. No special alarm was flashed, but military units around the globe were ordered on the alert for possible external attack or internal uprising. More than 500 intercontinental ballistic missiles (ICBMs) were in their silos or poised on launching pads. Half the Strategic Air Command's 1,280 medium and heavy bombers warmed up on runways. Others already were in the air heading toward preassigned targets. Antiaircraft missiles and fighter planes were deployed to take off points. And under the sea, ten Polaris submarines, each with sixteen nuclear-tipped rockets, prowled at the ready.

Hurrying into the White House, Bundy sent a radio message to a plane out over the Pacific carrying Secretary of State Dean Rusk, five other cabinet members and their aides toward a meeting with the Japanese cabinet in Tokyo. Then he immediately set to work drafting positional papers for the new President.

One hour out of Honolulu, the Bundy message clacked to life the teletype machine in the plane's tiny radio room. A crewman tore it off and handed it to Rusk. Almost unbelieving, the Secretary read the words and rushed back to the main cabin to tell the others: Secretary of Treasury Douglas Dillon, Secretary of Commerce Luther Hodges, Secretary of Agriculture Orville Freeman, Secretary of Labor W. Willard Wirtz and Secretary of Interior Stewart Udall. Also aboard was the familiar bulk and half-chewed cigar of Press Secretary Pierre Salinger, who had ascended with John Kennedy from the Senate to the White House.

A pleasant businesslike trip to the Orient now became a nightmare of anguish and anxiety. Several on that elite passenger list walked numbly back to tell their wives. Some hovered about the radio room waiting. Some prayed. Some cried. Thousands of miles from Dallas, thousands of feet over the Pacific, more than half of John Kennedy's cabinet felt helpless and numb. They knew the President had been shot; they didn't know how seriously.

More messages, some of them conflicting, activated the typebars of the teletype. Word that he was receiving blood transfusions sounded encouraging. Word that he had been shot through the head sent their spirits plummeting again. Even then, there was a wisp of hope.

"I know a man can live when he is shot through the head

because I had that experience," said Orville Freeman. He told about his own ordeal as a Marine officer. On a combat patrol in Bougainville his jaw was shattered by a Japanese sniper's bullet. It meant eight months in the hospital and learning to talk all over again, but he had lived.

As the messages coughed in, the six cabinet members went into informal conference, with Rusk presiding. They decided that regardless of Kennedy's condition the plane would be turned around and, after a fuel stop at Honolulu, head for home. Rusk and Salinger would leave the party in Honolulu to fly to Dallas, while the others went on to Washington.

Then came the shattering news of the President's death. The entire party now would fly to Washington. During the brief fuel stop in Honolulu, only Salinger and Rusk left the plane— Salinger to read a statement on behalf of the six cabinet members to the waiting photographers and reporters, Rusk to slip away to telephone Washington.

Throughout the eight-hour, non-stop flight to the capital, the six key Kennedy leaders tried to look into the future, to divine Johnson's plans and desires. All felt it their duty to submit resignations, so as to give the new President a free hand, but correctly guessed that they would not be accepted. But no matter how hard they tried to look ahead, they could not keep from looking back, back on very personal memories of the young leader who had summoned them to the front lines of the New Frontier, who now lay dead in Dallas....

And to the remarkable clan called the Kennedys, to the millionaire father once prominent in the New Deal and world diplomacy, to the mother renowned for her beauty and tea-pouring energy in political campaigns, to the son who was Attorney General of the United States, to the son who was the youngest member of the Senate of the United States, to the style-setting sisters, to their glamorous husbands, to the whole dynamic, football-playing, theater-going, party-throwing, pool-pushing, child-rearing family—the black word came in a variety of ways and a variety of places.

Bobby Kennedy was lunching at Hickory Hill, his estate in nearby McLean, Va., with Robert Morgenthau, U.S. Attorney for New York's Southern District, and Morgenthau's chief

19

deputy, Silvio Mollo. The day was so pleasant Ethel Kennedy decided to serve the clam chowder and tuna fish sandwiches out on the patio.

At 1:15 P.M. a maid approached the table. "Mr. J. Edgar Hoover," she said, "is on the White House phone." At the same moment a workman in coveralls appeared in the doorway. "It says on the radio that the President was shot."

Bobby picked up a telephone extension on a little stand a few feet away. His hand rose compulsively to his mouth in profound anguish. Ethel went to his side and put her arms around him. It was nearly 15 seconds before he could say, "Jack's been shot. It may be fatal."

He and Ethel went into the house to seek more information on a private extension. And several calls later, Robert F. Kennedy reappeared in the living room and uttered but two words: "He died."

And then he set off by himself. He paced the lawn in silence for a long time, head down, hands in pockets, followed only by Broumis, his big black Newfoundland dog. Suddenly he stopped. Now he was in control again. Now he set about organizing things in the galvanic family way that was a Kennedy trademark. Ethel and Dean Markham, a Harvard classmate who hurried over, were dispatched to pick up the children, scattered in three schools. Teddy Kennedy and Eunice Shriver were sent flying to Hyannis Port to the side of their parents, who now had lost three of their nine children.

When his children arrived, Bobby gathered them out on the lawn and told them in what words he could muster. Seven-year-old David broke down in tears and buried himself in his father's arms.

Teddy Kennedy was presiding over a half-empty Senate chamber. Richard Riedel, a press liaison officer, spotted the dark bulletin on the Associated Press wire in the press gallery. He darted onto the floor, where Sen. Winston Prouty (R-Vt.) was holding forth on a bill for federal library services. Riedel whispered to Sen. Spessard Holland (D-Fla.), the first senator he met, then to Sen. Wayne Morse (D-Ore.), sitting in the leader's seat managing the bill. Spotting Teddy up on the dais, Riedel immediately rushed up and whispered in his ear, "Senator, your brother has been shot." Teddy gasped. "No!" Gathering up a fistful of papers, he left the chamber at once.

As senators hurried from their offices to the floor, stunned by the death of their chief executive and former colleague, Senate Chaplain Frederick Brown Harris mounted the rostrum. "We gaze at a vacant place against the sky, as the President of the Republic goes down like a giant cedar." Then he consoled them with the words spoken on the morning of Abraham Lincoln's death, 98 years ago, by Rep. James Garfield of Ohio, who was himself to fall to an assassin's bullet 16 years later: "God reigns and the government lives at Washington."

Sen. Mike Mansfield (D-Mont.) was too stunned to ask for a motion of adjournment. The task fell to the minority leader, Everett Dirksen of Illinois. In the confusion, no reason was given in the official records. The Senate of the United States simply stopped.

At the opposite end of the Capitol, House Speaker John McCormack of Massachusetts, 71, was bent over a plate of ice cream in the House restaurant, little realizing that he was now next in line for the presidency. Two newsmen approached with the news. McCormack's spoon clattered to the table. "My God! My God! What are we coming to?" he cried for an entire nation. He hurried out to the press gallery to read the story rolling in over the AP ticker. As his first official act as the ranking executive in Washington he ordered all government flags

dropped to half mast. Within minutes, a Secret Service guard fell in behind him and two agents took up positions outside the door of his Washington hotel suite.

At the Supreme Court, the nine justices were conferring behind closed doors. An aide knocked on the heavy oak door. The word stunned the whole court. Chief Justice Earl Warren, who had administered the oath of office to John Kennedy, ended the conference immediately.

There were the other Kennedys to be told . . .

Joan Kennedy, Teddy's handsome blonde wife, was having her hair done at Elizabeth Arden's in Washington. None of the girls in the salon could summon the courage to tell her. So, still unknowing, she walked down the street and there at the edge of a crowd gathered around a television set in a store window, she heard of the murder of her husband's brother.

In Jefferson, Wis., Rosemary Kennedy, the President's sister, heard the news over television in the day room of St. Collet's School for the Retarded, where she has lived for many years. "She understood," said a nurse.

The news was kept from 98-year-old Mrs. John F. Fitzgerald, the President's maternal grandmother. "What would be the use of telling her at her age?" said her son, Thomas Fitzgerald.

In the Kennedy compound at Hyannis Port, home grounds of the family touch football team and the ferocious guest-baiting parlor games of wit and knowledge, preparations already were underway for the big two-turkey family feast on Thursday. By tradition, the family always came home for Thanksgiving. It didn't matter whether you were a Senator, Attorney General or President of the United States, you were expected home for Thanksgiving.

Rose Kennedy had just returned from the country club golf courses when niece Ann Gargan, in tears, rushed in. The news hit her like a giant wave, but she managed to keep her head held high, in the way her children always admired when tragedy struck. There and then she decided not to awaken her napping husband, invalided with a stroke since December, 1961. Instead, she asked his Boston doctor if the 75-year-old invalid could stand the shock. The doctor said he could, but she decided to wait until morning. That night Joseph Kennedy was talked out of television in favor of watching a long movie on his home screen. He retired as usual at 9:30 P.M., enjoying the luxury of ignorance denied the rest of the world.

On that night of strange comings and goings at the White House, of whispered conferences and hurried footfalls in the corridors, Caroline and little John Kennedy were taken to the home of their maternal grandmother, Mrs. Hugh Auchincloss. There, they learned for the first time that the big smiling man who played horsey with them in his rocking chair and let them romp in his big oval office would not be home for their birthdays, and they learned why.

* * * *

LYNDON JOHNSON sped unannounced to Love Field ahead of the white hearse carrying Jacqueline Kennedy and the President's body. On orders from Brig. Gen. Godfrey McHugh, Kennedy's Air Force aide, Air Force One and the almost identical vice presidential plane had been taxied to a secluded spot on the opposite side of the field, away from the busy terminal complex. Four seats in the rear compartment of the presidential jet, a small cabin normally occupied by White House assistants, had been removed to make room for the casket. Stepping past the vice presidential plane—a huge step in history—Johnson boarded Air Force One and went immediately to the private presidential bedroom.

Shortly before 2 P.M. the hearse pulled up at the rear door of the plane. The casket was lifted aboard and maneuvered down a narrow corridor beside the presidential galley into the rear compartment. With the four seats removed, the only furnishings were a desk and two chairs side by side on the right hand side. Mrs. Kennedy eased herself into the right seat nearest the bronze coffin. Around her stood Gen. McHugh and three of Kennedy's closest friends, Kenny O'Donnell, Larry O'Brien and Dave Powers, who had come with him all the way, from Boston Common to 1600 Pennsylvania Avenue.

The plane had been standing in the glaring Texas sun more than two hours and the cabin was sweltering. O'Donnell instructed McHugh to get the plane into the air. The two fan jet engines on the starboard wing roared to life, then suddenly died. McHugh raced to the pilot's cabin to find out what had happened. Pilot Col. James Swindal told him assistant White House press secretary Malcolm Kilduff had ordered the plane held up to await the arrival of Mrs. Johnson and a federal judge who was coming to administer the oath of office to Lyndon Johnson.

For the first time Mrs. Kennedy and the few close friends gathered around the casket in the tail of the plane learned that the new President was aboard Air Force One, a few feet away. The crew had assumed everyone knew Johnson was behind the closed doors of the presidential bedroom. Mrs. Kennedy and her companions in sorrow knew he was at Love Field but had assumed he was aboard the Vice President's plane.

In their grief and shock, those closest to the fallen President had overlooked the full implications of the automatic transfer of government power, the passing of the torch to a new President. This beautiful plane, with paintings and other decorations personally selected by Jack and Jackie Kennedy, no longer was theirs to command. Lyndon Johnson rightfully occupied the very private presidential sanctum with its desk, easy chairs and twin beds. There at his elbow was the telephone that could connect him, through the plane's complex communications apparatus, with any sector of the globe. Already, Lyndon Johnson was using that phone. It was the one instrument at hand that enabled him to take a quick, firm grip on the reins of government.

It was 30 minutes before Lady Bird Johnson arrived with U.S. District Judge Sarah T. Hughes, 67, a tiny, kindly faced woman whom Kennedy had appointed to the judiciary in 1961. Johnson asked Mrs. Kennedy to join him in the large gold upholstered conference room amidship for the oath taking. Leaving McHugh to stand vigil over the body, the widow walked forward with O'Donnell, Powers and O'Brien. Twenty-seven people crowded into the cabin, making conditions even more stifling. Among them was Rear Adm. George Burkley, President Kennedy's personal physician, his shirt cuffs still stained with blood, his one mission in life cruelly ended. Judge Hughes read the oath in a frail voice barely audible above the whine of the jet engines, which had begun to warm up again.

Holding the small leather-bound Bible which John Kennedy had kept in his aft sleeping compartment, Johnson raised his right arm and repeated the words softly: "I do solemnly swear that I will faithfully execute the office of the President of the United States, and will to the best of my ability preserve, protect and defend the Constitution of the United States. So help me God."

The time was now 2:38 P.M., Friday, November 22, 1963. In the 188th year of the American dream and the 1037th day of the

New Frontier, the United States had a new President, its 36th President. John Fitzgerald Kennedy had been dead 98 minutes.

President Lyndon Johnson now turned to his tearful wife and kissed her on the forehead. He put his arm around Mrs. Kennedy and kissed her lightly on the cheek. Mrs. Johnson took the widow's hand in her own and said, "The whole nation mourns your husband."

"God bless you, little lady," said Dallas Police Chief Jesse Curry, "but you ought to go back and lie down."

"No, thanks, I'm fine," said Jacqueline Kennedy.

Andrew Johnson had taken the oath of office in a Washington hotel room; Chester A. Arthur, in his Manhattan town house; Theodore Roosevelt, in a Buffalo home; Calvin Coolidge, by lamplight, in the parlor of his father's Vermont farmhouse. And Lyndon Johnson in the sweltering cabin of an airplane.

Three minutes after he took the oath, President Johnson issued his first order as chief executive of the United States:

"Now let's get airborne."

* * * *

"I don't know if it means anything, but I'm missing a man, a young fellow named Lee Oswald," said R. S. Truly, manager of the Texas Book Depository Building, to a policeman. The alarm went out: pick up Lee Harvey Oswald. Male. White. About five-foot-six, 150 pounds, 24 years of age. Dark hair. Wearing dark jacket....

Somehow, Lee Harvey Oswald had slipped out of the book building. He walked about seven blocks to Griffin Street and tapped on the door of a Marsalis Street bus stalled in traffic.

It was now 12:40 P.M., ten minutes after the shooting. This wasn't a regular stop, but driver C. J. McWatters opened the door anyway. Oswald took the third seat from the front on the right. There were only five other passengers. At Houston and Elm Streets, Oswald would get a good view of the assassination scene, but the bus stalled in traffic again.

A driver up ahead jumped out of his car and ran back to tell someone, anyone, the astonishing news coming over the radio. "The President's been shot!" he hollered up at the bus driver.

Oswald said nothing. He asked for a transfer and got off. It was now 12:44 P.M. Crossing the street, Oswald hurried two blocks south to Commerce Street, jumped into a cab parked at the Greyhound Bus Depot. "Take me to 500 North Beckley." This was five blocks beyond his rooming house at 1026 North Beckley.

"What the hell you think happened out there?" asked the cabbie, William Whaley. Oswald didn't tell him.

It was now 1 P.M. Oswald paid the 95 cent fare, left the driver a nickel tip and backtracked the five blocks to his room. The housekeeper, Mrs. Earlene Roberts, was watching the assassination news on television, but she looked up as he ran in.

"You sure are in a hurry," she said.

He sure was.

Oswald changed his dark jacket for a light colored one. He left without a word. Walking south and east, he reached 10th Street between Denver and Patton by 1:30 P.M. He was now about halfway on a straight line between his room and the apartment of a man named Jack Ruby. Some people would make much of this later.

bout this time, Mrs. Helen Markham was waiting for a
. She saw a police car halt down the street. Officer J. D. Tip-
got out. He went toward a man whom Mrs. Markham
embers as being about 30 with a white coat and bushy
. The man pulled his gun and fired. Tippitt dropped, dying.
man strolled off, clearing his gun of spent shells. "Call
police! Call the police!" a woman screamed. Someone did,
Tippitt's radio.

I thought he was going to shoot me, too," Mrs. Markham
.

an auto salesman, Ted Callaway, saw a man running by
h a pistol in his hand. He had heard the shooting and
ing. And a little while before, he had heard about the Presi-
t's death.

'Man, what's going on?" Callaway yelled at the hurrying
re. The man mumbled something and kept on going, tak-
a right on Jefferson. But Callaway had gotten a good look.
t night he picked a man out of the police lineup. His name?
Harvey Oswald.

Six blocks away Johnny Brewer, a shoe store salesman, saw
nan duck into his doorway. A police car, siren screaming,

sped by, then made a U-turn and started back again. After it
passed, the man walked into the Texas Theater. Cashier Julie
Postal didn't notice he hadn't bought a ticket. She was too
distracted listening to an account of the President's assassination. About a dozen people inside were watching a movie
called "War Is Hell."

Brewer had followed the man across the street. He told the
theater cashier to call the police. When they arrived, he walked
up onto the stage. The house lights came up and the film
stopped. Brewer pointed to a man in the middle section halfway down. The man stood up.

Officer M. N. McDonald moved toward him and the man
shouted, "This is it!" He reached for his gun. McDonald
grabbed him and they wrestled between the seats. McDonald
got a hand on the butt of the pistol as the man squeezed the
trigger. The hammer clicked harmlessly on a faulty cartridge.
It took four more policemen to subdue him.

As the officers hustled their prisoner outside, the crowd
there yelled, "Kill him! Kill him!"

"I protest this police brutality," said Lee Harvey Oswald.
It was now about 2 P.M. The President had been dead offi-
cially one hour.

The President dead? Officer Tippitt dead? "I haven't shot anybody," the prisoner shouted as he was led handcuffed into police headquarters.

Police rapidly pieced together a case. Within an hour of the arrest, they made a paraffin test of Oswald's hands and face. Both were positive, they said. He had recently fired a gun, they said.

Back in the sixth floor of the book building, police found a rifle behind a stack of books diagonally across from the window through which the assassin had fired. Near the window they found three empty cartridge shells. These matched the rifle, a 6.5 mm Mannlicher-Carcano. They traced the gun to a New York importer, then to a Chicago mail order house, Klein's. Records there showed that the gun had been sold in March, with a four-power scope included, to an A. Hidell in Dallas for $19.95.

A. Hidell? A. Hidell? That was the same name found on an identification card in Lee Harvey Oswald's wallet, police said.

Meanwhile, police learned that Oswald was married, to a girl from Russia. Marina Oswald was located at Mrs. Paine's house. Mrs. Oswald admitted her husband had a rifle. And on Mrs. Paine's telephone pad police found the address of an O. H. Lee. This led police to Oswald's rooming house. In the room, they found the Dallas street map Mrs. Paine had given Oswald to help in his job-hunting. The map was marked with "Xs" outlining the route of the President's motorcade. And a line had been drawn on it, a line that approximated the path of the bullets that killed the President and wounded the governor. And there in the room was a holster. Police slipped the .38 pistol they had found on Oswald into the holster. Perfect fit. In the room, too, there was a photograph of Oswald holding an Italian rifle and a .38 pistol.

There was more, investigators said. A brown fiber found on the stock of the rifle matched Oswald's clothing. His palm print was on the metal underside of the rifle. His fingerprints were on cartons placed around the window.

Police also found the brown wrapping paper. They appeared to have found everything but the curtain rods.

* * * *

... A great shadow fell on the land and in the perspective of death there was a great slowing down and a great stopping. The farmer summoned to the house did not find the will to return to the field, nor the secretary to the typewriter, nor the machinist to the lathe, nor the wife to the dishes, nor the judge to the bench, nor the carpenter to the saw. There was a great slowing down and a great stopping and the big bronze gong sounded and a man shouted the market is closed and the New York Stock Exchange stopped, just stopped. The Boston Symphony Orchestra stopped a Handel concerto and started a Beethoven funeral march and the Canadian House of Commons stopped and a dramatic play in Berlin stopped and the United Nations in New York stopped and Congress and courts and schools and a race track in Rhode Island and a race track in Maryland and a race track in New York stopped, just stopped. And football games were cancelled and theaters were closed and in a town called Dallas a night club called the Carousel was closed by a mourner called Jack Ruby. . . .

* * * *

At 2:47 P.M. Air Force One lifted from the runway at Love Field and for the first time the name Lyndon Johnson figured in the "wheels up" bulletins filed by reporters who cover the arrivals and departures of the President. Climbing to 41,000 feet, above the turbulent Texas air drafts, Col. James Swindal leveled off the big bird and sent her hurtling toward Washington at 635 miles an hour. In the private presidential bedroom, Johnson set to work preparing a brief statement to be read upon arrival in Washington. In a forward compartment, Maj. Gen. Chester Clifton, Kennedy's military aide, messaged ahead to make arrangements for arrival ceremonies at Andrews

Air Force Base and the removal of the body to Bethesda Naval Hospital.

Mrs. Kennedy sat at the desk across the aisle from her husband's casket in the tiny rear section. Kenny O'Donnell, Dave Powers, Larry O'Brien and Godfrey McHugh stood around her, a corporal's guard of the faithful trying desperately to think of something soothing to say. At one point Mrs. Kennedy indicated the empty chair beside her and urged O'Donnel to sit down. He did so, but only briefly. The steady whine of the engines cut through the self-conscious silence, mercifully drowning out the stifled sobs and the heavy breathing of anguish.

Through it all, Jacqueline Kennedy maintained her composure. There were tears in her eyes and her features had gone pale with grief, but she did not give way to uncontrolled sobbing. Instead, she began talking quietly, feelingly about her husband to his friends. She talked about what a wonderful man Jack Kennedy had been; what a wonderful father he had been. Instinctively, she talked about things to be done in the days ahead. She vowed she would conduct herself in a manner that would have made him proud of her. And she spoke of arranging a dignified but impressive funeral, simple yet befitting the high office of the presidency, the kind of funeral she thought her husband would have approved of.

Discussion of funeral plans became more specific. Recalling her husband's love of football and his plan to attend the Army-Navy game in Philadelphia, she suggested that units from West Point, Annapolis and the Air Force Academy march in the funeral procession. Because her husband was a Navy man and proud of it, Mrs. Kennedy and his friends wanted a Navy ambulance to meet the plane at Andrews and take the body to the hospital. Forthwith, a call went out from Air Force One to the U.S. Naval Hospital at Bethesda.

And, incredibly, from the Bethesda end of the line, from one tiny voice in one tiny corner of the massive bureaucracy John Kennedy had headed until a few hours ago, there came an objection: there was, the man in Bethesda said, a Navy regulation against carrying caskets in an ambulance. The man in Bethesda was told in forceful language not recorded for history that he had better forget about the regulation, that he had better make certain the ambulance met the plane.

During the flight, Mrs. Kennedy decided the body would not be taken to a private funeral home; that a funeral director would be asked to go to the hospital to embalm the body there. This was done.

Less than an hour out of Washington, Johnson got on the plane's special radio telephone and placed a call to Mrs. Rose Kennedy in Hyannis Port. "I wish to God that there was something I could do," he told her. "I just wanted you to know that." He handed the phone to Lady Bird. "We feel like the heart has been cut out of us," she sobbed. "Our love and our prayers are with you."

Then he placed a call to Dallas, to Nellie Connally, wife of the seriously wounded Texas governor. "We are praying for you, darling, and I know everything is going to be all right, isn't it," he said in his folksy Texas style. "Give him a hug and a kiss for me."

The sun died in the portside windows of Air Force One, and somber shadows moved across its golden interior. On through the gathering gloom the big jet sped, with its precious cargo of human tragedy and national renewal. In the aft cabin, the body of a dead President. In the forward cabin, a new President on the phone binding the nation together again. While a widow sat with her hand resting lightly on the coffin, a new hand reached out to soothe the stricken soul of the Republic.

Dusk had fallen and a slim quarter moon was climbing a cloudy sky as Air Force One touched down at Andrews Air Force Base, where John Kennedy had returned many times from many places. Now TV cameramen turned off their flood lamps so as not to blind the pilot, and the big blue and white bird came up to the landing apron wailing like a banshee, the old Irish harbinger of death. In the sudden darkness, a yellow catering truck with fork lift platform used to raise food trays lumbered up to the rear door. Lights blazed on again, cruel in their starkness, and the big plane with "United States of America" lettered on it now looked not proud, not invulnerable but like a forlorn eagle.

Bobby Kennedy bounded up the steps. Behind the honor guard, rigid at attention, the gray Navy ambulance stood waiting. Eight pallbearers went up to receive the coffin, but the red-eyed, tight-lipped young men who had ridden with the body from Dallas decreed otherwise. They would be the honor guard; they would carry the casket. The chief could lean on them one last time.

And so it happened that the oldest of old friends, Kenny

O'Donnell and Larry O'Brien, Dave Powers and Godfrey McHugh, tenderly lifted the body of their fallen comrade to the bed of the fork lift truck. The coffin weighed more than half a ton, but they needed only two military men to help them.

As always, Jacqueline Kennedy elected to stay by her husband's side. She rode down with the coffin on the platform of the fork lift truck and declined the offer of a waiting limousine. With Bobby and McHugh she climbed unaided into the ambulance behind the casket. There were no seats in the crowded rear compartment, so the three of them made the ride to Bethesda Naval Hospital sitting on the floor, arms braced against the coffin of the late President.

A nervous and shaken Lyndon Johnson moved out of the shadows to grip the hands of waiting government officials and solemnly made his way toward the bank of microphones to read the message he had written on the plane. His message was brief, his words humble and imploring: "I will do my best. That's all I can do. I ask your help and God's."

Red lights blinking in the moonlit gloom of that incredible night, a helicopter rose over the bare tree tops and carried the new President and his First Lady to the south lawn of the White House.

In the coldly forbidding white-tiled morgue at Bethesda, under the bright hard glare of overhead lights, the body of John Fitzgerald Kennedy is given a painstaking post-mortem. It is X-rayed completely for any evidence of more bullets or

metal fragments, and vital organs are studied to determine the exact cause of death. A private funeral director prepares the body for burial, and the embalmed remains are placed in a new mahogany casket. Some of the handles and ornaments on the bronze one that carried the body from Dallas had been damaged en route.

Alone with her grief in a 17th floor suite of the hospital, Jacqueline Kennedy thought about the future. Her husband had lived in a world of heroes. History meant people to him, not events, and he had lovingly profiled his own special heroes in a Pulitzer Prize-winning book that portrayed the lonely figures who dared to buck popular opinion. She determined that his death would be remembered as a hero's death; his funeral, a hero's funeral; his grave, a hero's grave. There and then this remarkable woman, a heroine transfixed with tragedy but gallantly carrying on, worked out in amazing detail the plans for the extraordinary funeral that would bring a rare sense of majesty to her countrymen.

From the hospital, she asked artist William Walton to find a certain book on a certain shelf in the White House library containing sketches and photographs of Abraham Lincoln lying in state. Arthur Schlesinger, Jr., historian and White House adviser, and Richard Goodwin of the Peace Corps were sent immediately to the Library of Congress to do more research on the Lincoln rites. About the same time, Paul C. Miller, the Pentagon's funeral expert, hurried to the White

House with a copy of the newly revised "State, Official and Special Military Funeral Policies and Plans."

Sometime during the night, a White House limousine arrived at Bethesda and a chauffeur rode to the 17th floor with an overnight bag bearing the initials J.B.K. and a makeup case with the name "Mrs. John F. Kennedy." But she didn't change clothes.

Twenty minutes after the presidential jet set down at Andrews, Lyndon Johnson's helicopter eased onto its steel landing pad on the south lawn of the White House, within sight of Caroline's tree house and John-John's jungle gym. The new President, still in animated defense conversation with Bundy, Secretary of Defense McNamara and Under Secretary of State George Ball, strode up the lawn and through the flower garden. At the French doors leading into the President's oval office, he paused for a silent moment, then went in, alone.

For the first time he was there on his own, with all the awesome responsibilities of the office already crowding in on him. The room had an eerie quality of emptiness. Tearful secretaries already had cleared Jack Kennedy's desk of personal mementos: the coconut shell on which he had written a message for help when his PT boat was rammed by a Japanese destroyer in the South Pacific, the silver calendar recording the dates of the Cuban crisis, the framed pictures of Jackie and the children. In the Cabinet Room next door, staff aides had laid out pads and pencils for tomorrow's cabinet meeting and moved Johnson's chair to the head of the long table.

Johnson lingered only briefly in the White House, decided, instead, to work out of his old office on the second floor of the Executive Office Building across the way. Setting to work quickly, he called former Presidents Harry Truman and Dwight Eisenhower, enlisting their support during the difficult period of transition. Next he called FBI Director J. Edgar Hoover and ordered him to go all out in gathering evidence against the assassin. Congressional leaders of both parties trooped into the office and heard a plea for unity. Then various members of the White House staff came in to pledge their loyalty. A Filipino steward served dinner on a tray at his desk, while Johnson conferred with some of his old friends—George Reedy, Bill Moyers and Walter Jenkins—and set up more conferences for the next day.

At 9:24 P.M. Johnson left his office and was driven to "The Elms," his home in Washington's Spring Valley section. The handsome Norman-style mansion once belonged to Perle Mesta. In the hallway, he paused before a framed color photograph of his dear friend and fellow Texan, the late Sam Rayburn. The President saluted, then whispered: "Well, Mr. Speaker, I wish you were here tonight."

That night Johnson wrote his first two letters as President of the United States. They went to Caroline and John Kennedy, Jr. The President then summoned Secret Service Chief Jim Rowley to the house and told him of the heroism of agent Rufus Youngblood, who had shielded the Johnsons with his own body. "I want you to do whatever you can, the best that can be done for that boy," Johnson told Rowley.

Before retiring, the President sat with some close friends in his study and watched television. But when the screen showed films of John Kennedy shaking hundreds of outstretched hands in Dallas, he ordered the set turned off. "I just don't believe I can take that," he said.

And so, Friday, November 22, 1963, mercifully ended at long last.

* * * *

33

SATURDAY—November 23, 1963

THEY HAD waited silently all night outside the iron picket fence, their eyes scarcely leaving the lovely old house. Early in the evening the guards had kept them moving and so they walked slowly down the street, eyes right, and at the corner they turned and came back on the street side of the sidewalk. They looked like a strange group of mournful pickets, demonstrating not protest but love.

In the chill darkness before dawn, they were still there, now motionless, standing, staring across the broad lawn and through the bare elms at the house, at the softly lighted windows in the family quarters, at the black crepe lately hung over the door under the North Portico.

They saw the blinking red lights of the police cars up Pennsylvania Avenue and they knew this was the moment. The President was coming home. No sirens, no police whistles, no barking of orders that usually accompanied his return. At 4:22 A.M., Saturday, November 23, 1963, there seemed to be no sound on the street or in the land.

The gray Navy ambulance and the six black cars behind it paused at the northwest gate and turned in. And along the fence, men removed their hats and teen-agers removed their hands from the pockets of their jeans and women tightened their fingers around the pickets of the fence. Tears stained their faces, their young and their old faces, their white and their black faces.

At the gate the procession was met by a squad of Marines and led in along the gracefully curving drive between the elms. In days to come there would be larger and more majestic pro-

cessions but none so slow, none so geared to the rhythm of tears, as the cadence of the Marines this Saturday morning. In two straight lines, glistening bayoneted rifles held across their chests at port arms, they marched oh so slowly up the drive and all that could be heard was the sound of their shoes sliding on the macadam.

Under the portico, under the handsome hanging lantern, they stopped and divided and lined up with the soldiers and sailors and airmen on the sides of the steps, at the stiffest, straightest attention of their lives. Jacqueline Kennedy emerged first from the ambulance, still wearing the same pink suit stained through eternity the afternoon before.

With her husband's brother, the Attorney General of the United States, with his other brother, the youngest member of the United States Senate, with his sisters and his friends and aides whom he had led to this house, this far and now no farther, Jacqueline Kennedy waited in motionless silence while the flag-covered casket was removed from the ambulance. Then she and they turned in behind it and walked up the steps and through the glass doors and into the lobby and down the long corridor lined with stiff silent men in uniform and finally came to a stop in the East Room.

There the casket was laid gently onto a black catafalque like the one that held Mr. Lincoln on another dark incredible night almost one hundred years ago. There, the kneeling priests began praying as they and others would through the long day and night by the flickering light of the candles which silhouetted the honor guard riveted to the floor. In the great still silence, under the black draped chandeliers, one tried not to hear the mocking echoes or see the remembered sights, of Pablo Casals bowing the cello, of ballet dancers pirouetting, of great actors reading Shakespeare and Nobel scientists as ex-

cited as children by the house, of the Marine Corps quartet playing while the President and his lady danced and the great and the glamorous of the world danced in a gay swirl of coattails and long gowns.

But it was now 10 o'clock in the morning of a Saturday in another time and Jacqueline Kennedy, still sleepless, returned to the silent East Room. She kissed her husband for the last time and the casket was sealed. A few moments later she returned with the children and spoke to them quietly, trying to tell them something of the fact and the meaning of death. A fact and a meaning for which millions groped that day.

* * * *

In Hyannis Port, Rose Kennedy went to the seven o'clock Mass at St. Francis Xavier's Church, where Jack and the rest of the family always attended while staying at the Cape. The Mass was said on an altar donated by the Kennedys in memory of Lt. Joseph Kennedy, Jr., the Navy flier killed in World War II. A woman of strong faith, Mrs. Kennedy stayed for a second Mass and on the way out met Teddy Kennedy and Sargent Shriver hurrying up the steps to the eight o'clock Mass.

Back at the big gray-shingled house, the family faced up to the task of telling 75-year-old Joseph Kennedy that his second son, the one who had achieved the family dream, was now gone, too. Although he could neither talk nor write since the paralyzing stroke of two years ago, the old man indicated by his restlessness that he knew something was wrong.

He became particularly suspicious when his New York Times failed to appear in its regular place at the breakfast table. After a therapeutic session of wading in his indoor heated pool, he returned to his bedroom. He asked to have the television set turned on. Teddy, with an apprehensive glance at his sister Eunice, said the set wasn't working. The old man looked at his son, suspicion hardening. He pointed to the unplugged cord on the floor. Teddy looked at his father and saw his lie collapsing. With an abrupt movement, he re-inserted the TV plug, and, as the picture flickered into life, suddenly turned the set off. And now Teddy Kennedy told Joe Kennedy the worst.

The old man took the news with the same fortitude and toughness he had imbued in his children. And the television set was turned on again and there he remained all the long day, like millions of his countrymen.

* * * *

On his first morning as President of the United States, Lyndon Baines Johnson left his home at 8:40 A.M. under heavy Secret Service protection and reached the White House 15 minutes later. There, he conferred with Bobby Kennedy across a coffee table in the oval presidential office on the ground floor overlooking the rose garden. Then he walked with McGeorge Bundy and John McCone of the Central Intelligence Agency to the map-covered situation room and was briefed on the areas of crisis in the world. In the steady drizzle he strode briskly across the street and down an alley to the Executive Office Building for a 40-minute session with Secretary of State Dean Rusk in his old vice presidential office. Next, Secretary of Defense McNamara dropped by for a 50-minute conference, followed by key congressional leaders. It was nearly 11 by the time Johnson gathered up his wife and headed back to the White House, where they spent twenty minutes with Jacqueline Kennedy in the second-floor living quarters. Already, the big circular driveway on the Pennsylvania Avenue side of the house was lined with big black limousines carrying congress-men and diplomats, cabinet members and Supreme Court judges to view the casket on the catafalque in the East Room.

Former President Eisenhower came with his son John and Sen. Everett Dirksen. He waited for a moment under the drip-ping portico and then waited again in the Blue Room until President Johnson, first in the order of precedence, went in to pay his respects at the bier.

Together, Johnson and Eisenhower spent a half hour in silent prayer before the casket.

Shortly before noon, the Johnsons went across Lafayette Square to attend a memorial service at old St. John's Episcopal, the "Church of the Presidents." Then, after a luncheon with Eisenhower that included further discussion of world problems, the new President presided over his first cabinet meeting. He opened the meeting with a prayer and then asked all of them to continue to serve. "I need your help in the time ahead," he said.

Later that afternoon Johnson issued his first presidential proclamation, declaring Monday, the day of the funeral, a day of national mourning. He read it into a bank of microphones set up in the "fish room," lately stripped of its Kennedy me-mentos: the sailfish caught off Acapulco, the deer trophy bagged on the L.B.J. ranch. Standing before a large replica of the presidential seal, Johnson, in his quiet Texas drawl, told how he hoped the nation would observe the day of mourning:

"I earnestly recommend the people to assemble on that day in their respective places of worship, there to bow down in sub-mission to the will of Almighty God, and to pay their homage of love and reverence to the memory of a great and good man."

* * * *

The world grieved.

It grieved for a leader of liberty, a leader of reason, of patience and youth and promise. There was, it seemed, no Cold War this day, few enemies and no neutrals.

It was 10:55 P.M. and snow dusted the pavement of Red Square when Radio Moscow interrupted a program of classical music to announce that the President of the United States had been shot dead. The announcement was simple, no detail, no comment, no connection with the sins of capitalism, and Radio Moscow played funeral music until it went off the air at midnight.

A somber group of Russians waited for a bus in the snow on Gorki Street. They talked about Kennedy and their words reflected their own fears and uncertainty. "He was a good man," said a waitress. "It is always the good who suffer.". . . "Who will be the new President?" asked an engineer. "Is he a peaceful man?". . ."It is bad for the American people and for our people," said a student from the Technical Institute. "What might have happened if there had been another Presi-dent at the time of Cuba?"

Chairman Nikita Khrushchev cut short a tour of the Ukraine and hurried back to Moscow. He appeared at Spasso House, residence of the American ambassador, shortly after noon. Dressed in black and looking grim, he went to the condolence book which lay on a table near a photograph of Kennedy, framed in black. Slowly, almost ponderously, he affixed his glasses and, in a stillness broken only by the whirr of televi-sion cameras, he signed his name and the date, November 23, 1963.

Then Ambassador Foy D. Kohler took him by the arm and they went into a small, adjoining sitting room. They talked for 20 minutes. Mostly, Khrushchev reminisced about his first and only meeting with Kennedy, in Vienna, in 1961. After that meeting, the Russian premier had told aides: "I guess we scared that young man." A year later, Nikita Khrushchev and that same young man stood toe to toe on the edge of nuclear war and it was Khrushchev who backed off.

Fidel Castro was having lunch with French journalist Jean Daniel in the living room of the Cuban premier's summer home on Varadero Beach when news of the shooting came by telephone. They turned on the radio and heard that Kennedy was dead. Castro stood up. "Everything is changed," he said. "Everything is going to change. I'll tell you one thing: at least Kennedy was an enemy to whom we had become accustomed. This is a serious matter, an extremely serious matter."

Sir Alec Douglas-Home, prime minister of Britain, was en route to the English south coast for a weekend of relaxation with the Duke of Norfolk at ancient Arundel Castle. He turned around and drove back to London. "There are times in life," he said, "when mind and life stand still, and one such is now."

Queen Elizabeth II commanded her court into a week's mourning and, from 11 A.M. to noon on Saturday, the great tenor bell in Westminster Abbey, the final resting place of England's kings, tolled each minute, a token of tribute usually reserved only for the death of a monarch. This time it tolled for the great grandson of an Irish potato farmer.

Sir Winston Churchill, just turned 89 and the world's only honorary American citizen, and his lady Clementine sat up until well past 10 P.M., watching the tragedy unfold on television. "The loss to the United States and to the world is incalculable," rumbled the most famous and most inspiring voice of World War II.

Gay Paris heard it in mid-evening and the gaiety went out of it. Part of the expatriate American colony—businessmen, students, bearded artists from the Left Bank—stood in the drizzling rain on the Rue de Berri and watched a teletype machine in front of the New York Herald Tribune Building. It had been a long time since they felt so close to home—and yet so far away. Down the street, a pretty American blues singer leaned against a wall and cried. Mascara ran in dark streaks down her glistening cheeks. "It's not so hard to believe," she sobbed. "It's just so hard to take."

From the Elysee Palace, French President Charles de Gaulle, never one to give in to emotion, never one to place grief above duty, issued a simple tribute, de Gaullian in every phrase: "President Kennedy died like a soldier, under fire, for his duty and in the service of his country. In the name of the French people...I salute this great example and this great memory." He ordered the flag of France to half staff.

New Ross, County Wexford, Ireland, closed its shops and drew the window shades on its grief. Here in the ancestral home, where great grandfather Patrick Kennedy more than a century ago had begun the Kennedy odyssey to fame and fortune in the New World, he was known as Cousin Jack and they pointed with pride and a little awe to the cottage where his third cousin, Mrs. Mary Ryan, 62, "the Widow Ryan," had served him tea by the open fire only last June. Now, before the same fire, the Widow Ryan wept, comforted by her daughter Josephine and a priest. "My mother and I prayed for him," said Josephine. "It was all we could do."

Around the world, people lined up at American embassies to sign the condolence books. In the embassy in London they signed sheets of note paper and the embassy promised to have them bound and forwarded to the White House. Two Indian students labored for 20 minutes over their message. Their English wasn't very good and, at this of all times, they wanted to make sure they had it right.

The people who couldn't come called. Switchboards lit up and telephones rang in American embassies. In Moscow, it was Foreign Minister Andrei Gromyko calling Ambassador Kohler to express "shock and greatest sympathy to the American people." Elsewhere, it was also a clerk, a laborer, a house-

wife, calling anyone who answered just as long as the voice was American and they could tell him how they felt.

Tribute piled upon tribute; condolence upon condolence... "a giant of a man"..."a great President"..."a tragic loss"... "shocking"..."sorrow"..."grief"..."sympathy"...until the words, inadequate to begin with, began to wear from repetition.

In West Berlin they tried it another way.

It was nearly midnight in that island of freedom in the midst of the Communist world. The numbing news was more than three hours old. West Berlin felt particularly close to Jack Kennedy. Only five months before he stood hatless on the steps of the City Hall and electrified 150,000 Germans with the solemn pledge: "Ich bin ein Berliner" (I am a Berliner). And now, suddenly, he was dead. What could be done now for a fellow Berliner?

It began with less than a hundred students, gathering in the rain and darkness near the Technical University. Silently, on foot and carrying torches, they set out for City Hall, three miles away. At every corner, new marchers joined in. In 15 minutes, there were 3,000. Then there were 15,000 and more at every intersection. The only sound was the shuffling of feet. Torchlight reflected from the rain-slicked streets and glistened on tear-stained faces. And by the time they reached City Hall Square, there were now 60,000 people.

"The heavy loss suffered by our friends on the other side of the great water is also our loss," intoned sorrowing Mayor Willy Brandt. The Freedom Bell, a gift from the people of the United States to the people of beleaguered Berlin, began to toll slowly and mournfully from the City Hall tower and Horst Tammerman, 23, a mechanic, said: "We feel like our father has been taken from us. We feel the same grief. We feel left alone."

The entire cabinet of Katanga Province in the Congo dropped everything and collected their wives and rushed to the U. S. consulate. "We Bantus always mourn the passing of a great chief," explained one. And 3,000 half-naked tribesmen stood in silence for one minute in Kapsabet, Kenya. They had never heard of John Kennedy but leftist Home Minister Oginga Odinga had told them a great chief was dead.

It was early morning, Saturday, November 23, when the news reached the Far East.

Pandit Nehru, 74 years old and immensely wearied by years of trying to walk a neutral path and mediate between East and West, was asleep in New Delhi. Aides debated whether to waken him with the news. They decided to let him sleep until 6 A.M. Only the day before he had learned of a helicopter crash that killed five of his generals. "He has already had enough shocks for one day," an aide said.

The word came to Shiokawa, Japan, before dawn and someone ran to waken Mayor Kohei Hanami. Twenty years before, Hanami, then a 34-year-old lieutenant in the Japanese Navy, commanded the destroyer Amagiri (Heavenly Fog), on a dark August night when it rammed and sank PT 109, Lt. (JG) John F. Kennedy, commanding. "The world has lost an irreplaceable man," said Hanami, who with the impersonality of a warrior at war, once tried his best to kill him.

People did unusual things.

Striking employes of two Rio de Janeiro television stations went back to their jobs to transmit news of the tragedy; the ruling military junta of the Dominican Republic, unrecognized by the United States, decreed nine days of official mourning; Prince Norodom Sihanouk of Cambodia, who only hours before had proclaimed Communist China "Cambodia's best friend," ordered anti-American posters hauled down and a three-day moratorium on attacks on the United States.

Red China, implacably hostile even in death, heard the news in a bare 103-word broadcast. It was said that school children applauded and a diplomat from a neutral country reported that

a Chinese member of his staff commented cheerily: "That's good news. He was a very wicked man." The trade union paper, Kungjen Jih Pao, carried a cartoon of the slain Kennedy lying on his face and captioned it: "Kennedy Biting the Dust."

The word went out to far flung U.S. military bases and naval installations that the commander-in-chief was dead. Hardened soldiers, standing at attention, wept as the mournful notes of taps sounded across military posts. The flags of the U.S. Seventh Fleet in Tokyo Bay dipped in salute and tiny Japanese fishing boats sidled up to the great gray warships with their little flags at half mast, too. And this in the same bay where the Japanese had signed the surrender in 1945.

At dawn in civil war-torn South Viet Nam, there wasn't much time to mourn. Tears had to be wiped away quickly and the helicopters, flown by Americans and carrying Vietnamese troops, roared into the skies to carry on the intense and vicious jungle war against the Communist Viet Cong.

Down under, in Adelaide, Australia, American Dennis Ralston wanted to cancel out of the finals of the South Australian Tennis Championships. But U.S. Ambassador William Battle, a personal friend of the slain President, told him that Kennedy would have wanted him to go on. Ralston did. He lost.

Back home, the grief was more personal. Each mourned in the light of his own experience and conviction and those who had been against him in life were still against him but they mourned just the same, for a little piece of everyone died that afternoon in Dallas and, added up, they made a whole.

For Negroes, the comparison to Abraham Lincoln was inescapable. "One hundred years ago the emancipator, Abraham Lincoln, was struck down by an assassin's bullet," said A. Philip Randolph, president of the Pullman Porters' union. "Today, President John F. Kennedy, who was the second emancipator of black people...has been struck down by an assassin's bullet."

It was John Kennedy who had sent thousands of federal troops and marshals into Oxford, Miss., at the state university to guarantee admission of a single Negro student.

In a Harlem bar, the talk centered about the Kennedy civil rights bill, stranded somewhere in the Congressional maze, and President Lyndon B. Johnson—how strange the name and title sounded now—was examined nervously and the Negro bartender growled unhappily: "Let's see what your cracker President is going to do for you now."

The top American Communists, Gus Hall, Ben Davis and Elizabeth Gurley Flynn, called the assassination "the ultimate end of the rise of violence and terror in this land by racists and the forces of the ultra-right;" and in Phoenix, Ariz., Thomas L. Thompson, 33, took his gun and pumped two shots through the window of the local John Birch Society headquarters. "They killed my man," he told arresting police in the mistaken impression, shared by many at first, that ultra-conservatives were behind the slaying.

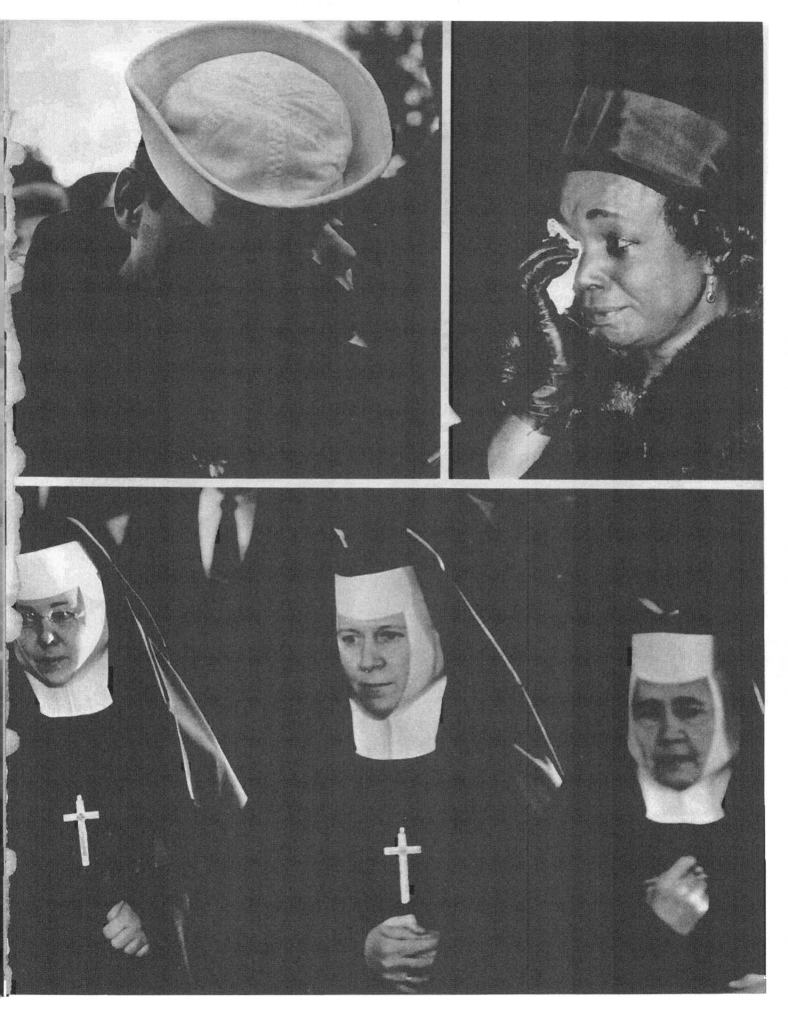

"My sympathy for the Kennedy family is no less than it is for the millions of people who have sustained equal losses in the fight for freedom," said former Maj. Gen. Edwin A. Walker, an apostle of conservatism.

Victor Lasky, author of the best-seller "JFK: The Man and the Myth," a book critical of the President, abruptly canceled a dozen lectures and three television appearances. "As far as I'm concerned," he said, "Kennedy is no longer subject to criticism on my part." His publishers withdrew the book from sale. And a salesman in Los Angeles stared moodily into his drink at a bar and said: "I didn't agree with him but, my God, he was our President."

"I guess this is part of growing up," said a Princeton senior, unhappy in his new-found wisdom. "Our parents have memories of Roosevelt's death and of Pearl Harbor, but this is the first time anything like this has hit our generation. We could laugh and make jokes about him but he was one of us."

Harvard quarterback Bill Humenuk heard about it on the practice field in New Haven where the President's old school team was getting ready to play traditional rival Yale the next day. "It's something you read about in history books and never think it's going to happen," he said. Harvard and Yale postponed their game for the first time since they started playing each other in 1875.

Virtually all games and programs of entertainment were called off for that weekend. The professional American Football League postponed its games but the National Football League decided to go through with its Sunday schedule and Ben Scotti and John Mellekas, teammates on the Philadelphia Eagles, got into a fist fight over it and both wound up in the hospital.

There were a few jarring notes among the eulogies and tributes but they were quickly suppressed.

A youth who identified himself as Rusty Wesson of Birmingham, Ala., called an "open mike" show at radio station WQXI in Atlanta and said: "Any white man who did what he did for niggers should be shot;" he managed to say this on the air before the announcer cut him off. A few school children in Dallas and Jackson, Miss., cheered the news, the cheers being part of a bitter inheritance.

Owen H. Reieson, 24, a red and black swastika on his left arm, celebrated "a miracle for the white race" in the rotunda of the state capitol in Madison, Wis., and police scooped him up into custody. Malcolm X, chief of the Black Muslim movement in New York, chortled, "chickens coming home to roost never did make me sad; they've always made me glad" and the faithful applauded but Elijah Muhammad, leader of the sect, promptly suspended him.

But these were tiny discords and they were engulfed by the solemn symphony of grief rising up from the nation and the world this day.

* * * *

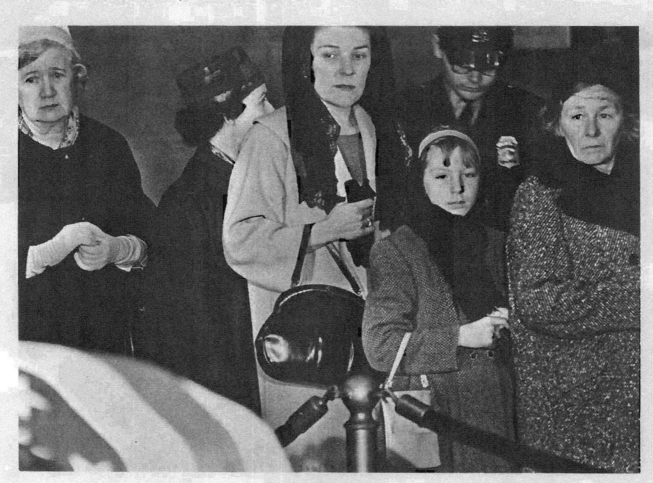

All that bleak and melancholy day, limousines rolled through the northwest gate of the White House, depositing distinguished mourners under the black-draped North Portico. An honor guard composed of representatives of the Army, Navy, Air Force and Marines stood at parade rest under the gracious swinging lantern, while Angier Biddle Duke, State Department protocol chief, helped the dignitaries from their cars. Slanting umbrellas into the downpour, reporters stood out on the leaf-flecked driveway watching the arrivals, as television cameramen huddled under plastic rain shields on camera mounts set up on the sodden lawn.

Former Presidents Eisenhower and Truman went in to pay their respects, as did Chief Justice Earl Warren, Gen. Maxwell Taylor and the Joint Chiefs, Ambassador Carl Rowan and practically the entire Cabinet, Supreme Court, Congress and diplomatic corps. New York's Gov. Nelson Rockefeller, the only announced candidate for President in 1964, came to view the flag-draped casket; so did Gov. George Wallace of Alabama, who had bitterly opposed the slain President over school integration. Striding somberly across the black rubber carpets in the hallway, House Speaker McCormack led a delegation of Congressmen into the East Room to offer a moment of silent prayer for their former colleague. Sen. Clair Engle (D-Calif.) recovering from a brain tumor operation, was wheeled in in a chromium wheelchair, his arm in a sling. Puffy-eyed and distraught, Sen. Hubert Humphrey (D-Minn.) wept unashamedly,

while the honor guard discreetly diverted their glances to their highly polished shoe tops.

All day long, while torrents of rain poured out of the somber leaden skies, a silent crowd gathered across the street in Lafayette Park to watch the procession of limousines rolling through the high iron gates. Too far away to identify any of the dignitaries, they huddled under the trees and relied on transistor radios to tell them who was coming and going. For a long time a lone picket paraded up and down the White House side of the street carrying a homemade sign that bore the strange inscription, "God Punished J.F.K." "How could you? How could you?" a woman, in tears, ran up screaming. Policemen made him move off to the other side of the square where the rain soon washed away most of his message.

And while the body of John Fitzgerald Kennedy lay in repose in the East Room, amid the flickering candles, the praying priests and the grieving friends, his imprint already was being removed from the house that he called home and office. Out in rain-swept West Executive Avenue two porters pulled a dolly loaded with models of sailing ships, paintings of famous sea battles, a globe of the world, a row of metal file cabinets. Over the rough cobblestones, on their way to a basement store room in the old executive office building, bounced the two rocking chairs on which the President of the United States had rocked while talking to world leaders and trying to ease his aching back. And all over the country heavy hearts bumped from cobblestone to cobblestone in the cruel rhythm of that moment.

* * * *

And in Dallas, police held Lee Harvey Oswald with a certainty that increased hourly. "This is our man," they said.

. . . Our man? Whose man was Lee Oswald? A product of what? How did he grow? Where was the twig bent? Could he have been helped? Did he cry out and did no one hear? . . .

Lee Harvey Oswald's mother was born Marguerite Claverie in New Orleans in 1907. She lost her mother when she was two but beyond that nothing much is known of her life until about the time of the 1929 crash when she married a stevedore, John Pic. She became pregnant two years later and Pic left her, she said, because he didn't want children. Their son John was born in 1932.

Divorcing Pic in 1933, she married Robert E. Lee Oswald, an insurance agent. In 1934 they had a son, Robert, Jr. In 1939 Mrs. Oswald became pregnant again but her husband never lived to see the child. He died of a heart attack two months before the birth of Lee Harvey Oswald on October 18. "I was left penniless with three boys," Mrs. Oswald said. She actually had $3,500 in insurance from her husband but that didn't stretch too far. She soon had to go to work. Her sister, baby-sitters, anyone she could get, cared for her infant son.

Finally, when Lee was three, she put him and his brothers into the Bethlehem Lutheran School, a boarding school for orphans or children with only one parent. "It was a wonderful religious education," said Mrs. Oswald.

. . . It was an education without a home, and not much of it proved lasting. As a grown man, Lee Harvey Oswald refused to join hands in grace at the table of a Quaker friend. He was now a proclaimed atheist. Ironically, it was his Russian-born wife, despite her years in the Soviet Union, who wanted their child baptized and she did it without his knowledge . . .

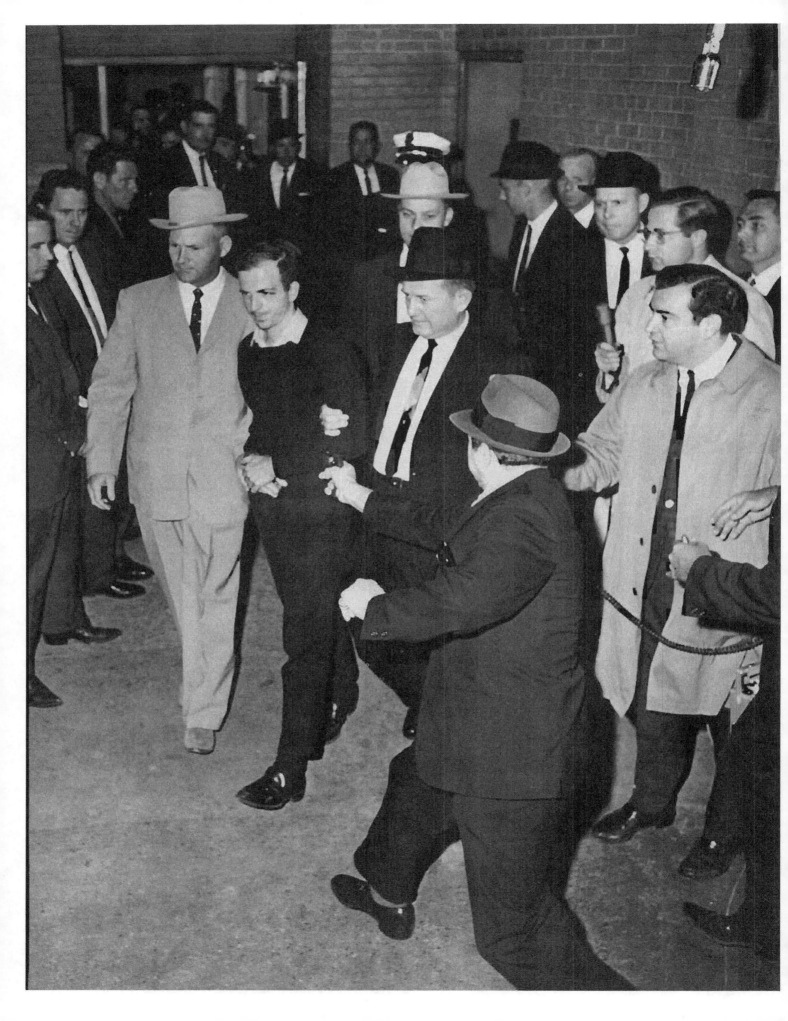

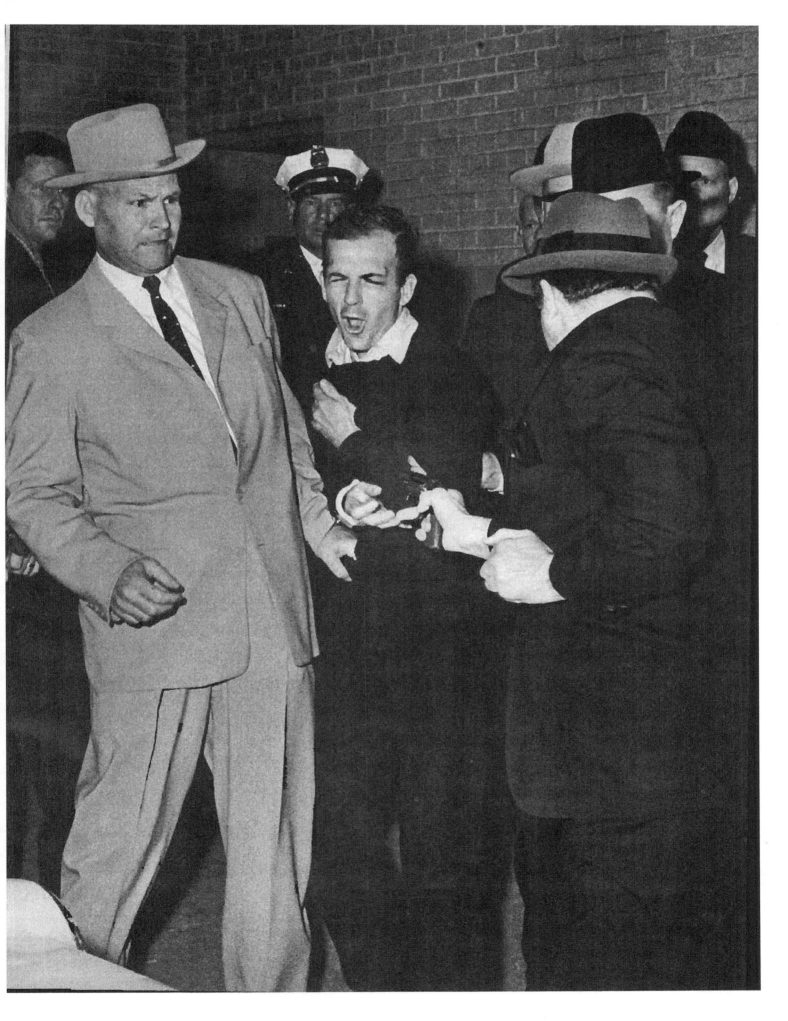

In 1945, when Lee was five, his mother married Edwin A. Eckdahl, a Boston electrical engineer who was working in the South. They sent the two older boys off to a Mississippi boarding school and took Lee with them to Fort Worth, Texas. In the spring of 1948, Eckdahl filed for divorce, claiming his wife had nagged unendingly about money, had hit and scratched him, had thrown a bottle and a cookie jar at him and once a vase, which caused him to duck so violently he wrenched and paralyzed his arm. "I had been married three times and altogether had husbands for a total of eight years," said the woman who now reverted to the name of Mrs. Oswald.

The two older boys were now returned home to Fort Worth to live with their mother and her youngest son. Lee Oswald liked to kibitz while his brother John played chess with a friend, Hiram Conway. Lee even learned enough about the game to beat them once in a while. But when he'd lose. . . .

"He'd throw the chess pieces all around and the older boys would try to hold him off," said Conway, "but he'd go kicking their shins and try biting their hands."

"That boy will be electrocuted or shot down some day," Hiram Conway used to say with the reckless hyperbole of youth.

But others had different memories. A fourth-grade teacher, Mrs. Emma Livingston, remembers how she tried to help Lee Oswald:

"I'm a real pushover for the underdog. Here was a boy who was having a hard time making grades. He couldn't spell, he couldn't read.

"I felt no necessity for helping the rest of the students because they were going to get help at home if they needed it. Everyone else had a mother or a daddy who was interested.

They had someone to depend on. Evidently Lee didn't.

"I helped him after school with his spelling. I remember how pleased we all were when he got an A on a spelling paper. It was the top paper during our next 'Open House.' For Lee an A was a real accomplishment."

Perhaps out of gratitude, or affection, Lee one day presented Mrs. Livingston with a puppy from his dog's litter. "After he left my class I was tempted to get rid of the dog but I was afraid that would be the straw that broke the camel's back.

"I thought he'd never amount to much in the world but wouldn't cause any real problems, either for himself or his neighborhood.

"Somebody, or a lot of somebodies, missed an awful lot of opportunities down the line. It is a rare child that will not respond to genuine concern and affection. Somebody along the way should have seen something. . . . I didn't."

. . . Somebody did see something, though. A man named Renatus Hartogs . . .

In August, 1952, Mrs. Oswald moved to New York to be closer to her oldest son, John Pic, who was then in service nearby and married. She brought Lee with her. On first glance, he was unremarkable: I.Q. 103 against an average of 100, an achievement mark of 7.4 in his last grade at Fort Worth—the sixth—against a norm of 6.5. A withdrawn solitary boy, he was enrolled in three successive schools but became a habitual truant.

Even when Mrs. Oswald would escort him to school, he'd dart away as soon as her back was turned and head home. "We all thought he was kind of queer," said a neighbor, Mrs. Gussie Keller. "He would play by himself with his toy guns and all you could hear was 'bang! bang! bang!' "

He soon came to the attention of juvenile authorities, his only youthful brush with the law and perhaps the one time when the bent twig could have been straightened. Dr. Renatus Hartogs, chief psychiatrist for the Youth House for Boys in the Bronx, examined Lee for four weeks in the spring of 1953.

This boy, Dr. Hartogs concluded, was potentially dangerous. He was given to violence and had fantasies concerning it. He had a hatred for authority, resented people who had fathers. Outwardly he was calm. But he was schizoid with an underlying, hidden, latent tendency toward aggression. This boy, the psychiatrist said, needed treatment. He didn't get it.

Lee Oswald was referred to two private institutions. Neither had room. A third was not set up to handle a case such as Oswald's. A fourth wouldn't take Lee unless his mother would cooperate.

"Please keep out of family affairs," Mrs. Oswald told John Carro, Lee's probation officer for nine months.

"His environment was poor because his mother was in need of help herself," Carro said. It was suggested that a male therapist might compensate for the boy's lack of a father. Nothing came of the suggestion.

To Carro, Oswald as a teen-ager was "a shy, introverted kid with a slight build and small features—pathetic but kind of likeable, a boy of average ability." This was a time when Oswald said of his schoolmates: "They don't like me and I don't like them." And of his mother: "She's my mother, I guess I love her, I guess I do."

"This kid was seeking acceptance, a sense of belonging, a feeling of identity that he didn't get here," said the probation officer. In the light of events of ten years later, John Carro had an afterthought: "Sometimes kids kill somebody just to let the world know they exist."

The wandering Oswalds left New York abruptly late in 1953 or early 1954 and returned to New Orleans. Officials at Beauregard Junior High School had no idea that four juvenile judges in New York had recommended that Lee receive psychiatric treatment, and probably would have been astonished had they known. For Lee attended classes regularly, seemed suddenly to have no discipline problems other than a few recess scuffles. He didn't like schoolmates to call him "Yank" because of his northern accent. His grades, 73 average, were just passing. But by the end of the next year, ninth grade, they averaged 77.

After ninth grade Lee transferred to a senior high school, Warren Easton. His personal history questionnaire shed some light on this quiet, shuttered boy. It noted the family had moved from the city's Lakeview area, a clean middle income neighborhood, to Exchange Place, a saloon-fronted street in the heart of the boisterous French Quarter.

Any close friends in Warren Easton? the questionnaire asked. "No," wrote Lee. The next question: "If so, name two." Lee Oswald had written in two names. Then they were erased. Desired vocation? Lee only checked "military service" and "undecided." Religion? "Luthan," he misspelled. Name of the church? No answer.

It really didn't matter much. Oswald dropped out of Warren Easton after only 23 days there. Not that his education had ceased. At the library, he began reading the masterwork of the architect of communism, "Das Kapital" by Karl Marx. Oswald never showed that he mastered the laborious tome but there was no mistaking its thundering conclusion: all is wrong with the world.

Here in a book of massive indignation addressed to the wretched of the world, the confused, rootless 15-year-old boy could finally find a cause, an explanation.

"It was like a very religious man opening the Bible for the first time," he said later.

His mother took his choice of reading philosophically. "He brought home books on Marxism and Socialism but I didn't worry. You can't protect children from everything—just try to help them see things in the right way. Besides, if those books are so bad why are they where any child can get hold of them?"

In September, 1956, a little after John Kennedy had made an unsuccessful try for the vice-presidential nomination, Mrs. Oswald moved to Fort Worth. Lee enrolled at Arlington Heights High School. He had always liked football and went out for the 'B' team. After practice, the boys were supposed to run a short sprint. Oswald refused.

"This is a free country and I don't have to do it," he said. Oswald was dropped from the team.

Shortly thereafter, on October 24, 1956, a week after he was 17, Lee Oswald showed he was beyond kid games anyway. He joined the Marines and reported to boot camp at Camp Pendleton, California.

. . . A Marxist Marine in the Cold War year of 1956? Did he want to fight his country's battles? Or just anybody? Was he running away or running toward? . . .

Allen Graf of Buffalo, N. Y., a barracks mate, recalled that Oswald talked about the tough times his mother had during the depression. "And he always said he hated the outfit."

The Marines trained Oswald in aviation electronics and then shipped him to Japan. He arrived in the Orient in July, 1957, where he won a good conduct medal and a private first class stripe. He lost the stripe when he was court-martialed for having an unauthorized pistol. By one account, the gun was discovered when he dropped it on the barracks floor and it fired. Oswald later told a friend it was no accident.

"That's one way to warn people to leave you alone," the friend said. "You bet," said Oswald.

Oswald was court-martialed a second time for using abusive language to non-commissioned officers.

Despite his almost constant smile, Oswald was a "real aggravator," said Peter Connor, who had served overseas with Oswald.

"When the fellows were heading for a night on the town, Oswald would remain behind or leave before they did. No one knew what he ever did." But one barracks mate recalled Oswald had begun using his spare time to study Russian. His thoughts were somewhat Russian, too. He thought it was "imperialistic" that American troops were stationed in Japan. In October, 1958, Lee Oswald came home to the United States and was assigned to Air Control Squadron 9 at Tustin, California, as a radar operator.

The following July he received a letter from his mother. She had been injured by a falling box at the store where she worked and her compensation case wasn't yet settled. She needed her son. He was given a hardship discharge September 11 and headed straight for Fort Worth.

"I had sold the furniture and was living on $3 a week," said Mrs. Oswald. "I don't think I will ever forget the shame I felt when my boy entered that small place with a sick mother."

He stayed three days, sleeping on a roll-away bed. Then he said: "Mother , my mind is made up. I want to get a ship and travel. I think I could earn more money for both of us." He left for New Orleans with $1,000 saved from the Marines. Two and a half weeks later Mrs. Oswald received a letter from Lee. He was on his way to Europe. On October 13, he arrived in Moscow. The disciple had entered paradise. "I'm through," he said

at the U.S. Embassy. "Capitalism has passed its peak. I've seen poor niggers and that was a lesson. People hate because they've been told to hate. It's the fashion to hate people in the United States."

He signed an affidavit in November saying "I affirm that my allegiance is to the Soviet Socialist Republic." The USSR didn't quite return the compliment. The government denied Oswald citizenship but permitted him to stay as an alien resident.

Priscilla Johnson, an American expert on Russia, had met other defectors and ran into Oswald in Moscow. "He was pleasant enough but helpless and lost. His intellectual grasp was secondary, his hostility was the strongest element. I soon came to feel that this boy was the stuff of which fanatics are made."

Back in Fort Worth, Mrs. Oswald read in a paper that her son had defected to Russia. Soon afterward the lady she was working for dismissed her. The sins of the son visited on the mother?

Lee Oswald took a factory job in Minsk. There he met a pretty pharmacist named Marina Nicholaevna. Six weeks later, in the summer of 1961, they married. Their circle of friends gradually melted away. The Russians didn't like Lee or trust him. In turn, he longed for the personal freedom he was used to as an American. He found himself boosting his country at informal gatherings. He also joined a rifle club. He had been an average shot in the Marine Corps—barely qualifying as sharpshooter and later slipping to the lowest category, marksman, by one shot.

Meanwhile, the Marine Corps, having learned of Oswald's defection, changed his discharge to "undesirable." Oswald was enraged. He wrote a letter of protest in January, 1962, to Navy Secretary John Connally demanding the Navy Department "take the necessary steps to repair the harm done to me and my family. I shall employ all means to right this gross mistake or injustice to a bona-fied (sic) U.S. citizen and ex-serviceman." He went on to describe himself as a fellow Texan "who had gone to the Soviet Union to reside for a short time (much in the same way E. Hemingway resided in Paris)." Connally, who had just resigned as Navy secretary, referred the letter to Washington where the Corps action was upheld. Connally would hear from Oswald again.

About that time Oswald wrote Texas Sen. John Tower. He said he had been trying without avail since July, 1960, to get an exit visa from the Russians for himself and his wife. "I beseech you, Senator Tower, to rise (sic) the question of holding by the Soviet Union of a citizen of the U.S. against his will and expressed desires." The State Department eventually decided Oswald had not become an expatriate and could come home. The U.S. Embassy loaned him $435.71 (later repaid) for passage for himself, wife, and their new daughter, June Lee, four months old.

On June 13, 1962, aboard the Holland-America liner Maasdam, the prodigal came home. There was no joyous, forgiving father to greet him, no family to welcome him. He came down the gangplank with a wife, baby, six suitcases and no money.

. . . And, one wonders, what else did Lee Oswald bring back? What plans, what notions? He had joined the Marines and found no identity. He had journeyed to Russia and found no paradise. Where could he go now? . . .

Spas Raiken of the Traveler's Aid Society met the Oswalds. "One thing that impressed me was that he was trying to avoid contact with anybody. It was like trying to pull teeth to get any information out of him."

One of Oswald's first acts on his return was to tell a lie. He said he had been on duty as a Marine guard at the Moscow embassy. He noted things were not as rosy in the Soviet Union as the propaganda would have it.

The Oswalds moved in with Lee's mother in Fort Worth. Lee spent a month looking for work without luck. "He wasn't bitter," said his mother. "He knew he had made a mistake in going to Russia and would have to pay for it."

Oswald finally landed a job and moved into a $59-a-month apartment with his family. By then, he had met some of the Russian-speaking community of the area. They asked the Oswalds to dinner several times. Everyone liked Marina, all the more so because of the way her husband treated her. He beat her for such crimes as forgetting to draw his bath, for wanting to smoke and wanting to learn English.

In a warm-hearted gesture, the friends brought clothing and a baby pen. Oswald frostily rejected them as "charity."

"He barked at me so many times I withdrew," said one man.

Once Oswald came home while some acquaintances were there, ignored them, ordered Marina to fix dinner and ate it with her while the guests waited. He spurned an offer by a man to teach his wife English—something she dearly wanted to learn. Oswald said he wanted her to speak only Russian so he could preserve his fluency. Indeed, he did speak fluent Russian but his grammar was bad.

The friends said Marina thought life in Minsk had been hard and she was pleased to be in the United States. Then, in September, her husband lost his job and moved into Dallas, to the Y.M.C.A., to look for work. He found a job with a print developing firm, rented an apartment and was soon joined by his wife and child. But then Mrs. Oswald abruptly moved out with the child because he was beating her. She stayed with friends for about two weeks and finally returned after he begged her repeatedly to come back. Before she did, however, she had her daughter baptized secretly.

In February of 1963, the Oswalds met perhaps the steadiest friend they were to have. She was Mrs. Ruth Paine, 31, former student at Pennsylvania University and Middlebury College, who was separated from her husband. Mrs. Paine lived in a four-room house in suburban Irving. As a student, she had studied Russian.

"I thought Marina a wonderful person. We were both young mothers and liked to talk about families and housework. I thought that I could teach her English and she could help me with my Russian. I didn't like her husband at all, though. It was almost as if he were daring you to like him and hoping you wouldn't."

Everett Glover, a chemist, invited the Oswalds over because a group of scientist friends of his were interested in learning Russian so they could read Soviet technical journals. They would be pleased to meet a couple who had recently lived in the Soviet Union.

But Oswald recited Marxist slogans rather than tell his experiences behind the Iron Curtain. "I don't even think he knew what they meant," said one guest. To Mrs. Paine, Oswald acted like a prophet handing down indisputable law. A prophet without honor in his own land.

Oswald was an uncommunicative worker at the print plant. And an incompetent one. In April, 1963, he was fired, which was no blow to his co-workers who had stared bug-eyed when he brought out a Communist newspaper at lunch hour. There was a lot of talk in Dallas about Communists and here, it seemed, was one in their own shop.

In May, Oswald, who had been subsisting on $33 a week unemployment compensation, decided to try New Orleans for work. Mrs. Paine took Marina, who was pregnant again, and the daughter into her home. When Oswald notified them that he had gotten a job May 10 as an oiler at a coffee warehouse, Mrs. Paine drove Marina and the little girl to New Orleans.

The Oswalds settled into a house, Lee took out a library card and things seemed stable — for the moment. When he wasn't reading, Oswald would be glowering around the neighborhood.

He was always coming home with stacks of books, said A. P. Eames, who lived nearby. "He was very arrogant in that he would not greet you or make any attempt to be congenial."

"When he passed me or my husband in the yard, he just kept walking with his head down," said his landlady, Mrs. Lena Garner.

Twice he plastered pro-Castro signs on the outside of the house. Mrs. Garner asked him to take them down. Oswald did. But he could get awfully sensitive about the Cuban leader.

Connie Kaye, a singer at Pat O'Brien's bar, once had a run-in with Lee Harvey Oswald. "I have a gag in my routine, something about 'Castro, that bastro.' Oswald came up to me. 'What are you using that line for? What are you mocking Castro for?' "

Not long afterwards, that same Oswald approached Carlos Bringuier, head of the New Orleans chapter of the Cuban Student Directorate, and offered to help train *anti*-Castro fighters. Bringuier was suspicious. He was astonished a few days later when he ran into Oswald on the street passing out "Fair Play for Cuba" leaflets. There was a scuffle. On August 12, a judge fined Oswald $10 for disturbing the peace.

As a result of the publicity, he wound up on a local TV program and fell all over himself trying to explain he was a Marxist, not a Communist, and what it all meant. His thinking was blurry, at best.

That was just what the State Department thought when, that June 25, it received an application from Oswald for a passport renewal for travel to Europe, Poland and Russia as a photographer. Although he swore he had "never sought or claimed the benefits of the nationality of any foreign state," and although files in Washington showed Oswald had a history of "fuzzy" Marxist thinking, the Department issued the passport.

The list of books he had taken out of the library wasn't exactly a model of consistent study, either. Or was it? "Portrait of a President" (a book about John F. Kennedy), several anti-Communist titles and a book describing the assassination of Huey Long.

On July 19, Oswald was fired from the coffee warehouse. His boss said he was "never around when we needed him." Four months later, less than a half dozen of the 100 or so employes at the plant could remember that he had ever worked there.

It was in September, that Lee Oswald began the long, twisted journey that would bring him to Dallas—and into history. On September 17, he got a 15-day tourist card from the Mexican consulate in New Orleans. He said he wanted to make a bus tour taking photographs. On September 23, Mrs. Paine, who happened to be passing through town, picked up Marina and her daughter, June, and took them back to Irving. Marina was now eight months pregnant. Mrs. Paine didn't know it then but she most probably was carrying, among the Oswald pieces of luggage, an Italian carbine wrapped in a blanket roll.

Early the next morning Oswald, himself, left. He left without paying the rent.

He had told the women he was going to Houston to search for work. Instead, he went to the Mexican border town of Nuevo Laredo, arriving September 26. That was the day the White House announced that President Kennedy would visit Texas. Before crossing the border, Oswald spent $32 on clothing (acquaintances had said his baby sometimes didn't have milk to drink) and took a bus the 750 miles to Mexico City. Oswald took a room at the Hotel Comercio, a place rarely frequented by Americans. He talked briefly to a maid and night watchman in bad Spanish.

He applied at the Cuban Embassy for a transit visa for the Soviet Union. He was told it would take time. Furious, he swept out the door, slamming it behind him. At the Russian Embassy, he was told such a visa might take three months. He slammed their door, too.

He left Mexico City, again by bus, October 2, and was in the United States the next day. He reached Dallas, probably by hitch-hiking, October 4. Mrs. Paine said she couldn't drive into town to pick him up because she had just given blood to

help pay for the birth of his baby, expected momentarily. Oswald thumbed his way to Irving, said hello and headed back to town, where he took a room at the "Y." That was the day Mrs. Paine gave him the Dallas street map which police later found in his room on North Beckley, a room he took several days after his return to Dallas.

The FBI, meanwhile, had checked from time to time on Oswald, had even talked to Mrs. Paine about him. But he wouldn't be included in the list of "risky" individuals in Dallas submitted to the Secret Service in advance of the President's arrival there.

"The only reason in his case: was he a spy or a saboteur? In Oswald's case there was absolutely no indication whatsoever," an FBI spokesman said. "There was nothing in his background to indicate he was going to do anything...."

On October 14, a Monday, some of the neighborhood girls in Irving were having a coffee klatsch. Among them were Mrs. Paine, Marina and Mrs. William Randall. They felt sorry for Marina, who was about to have a child, with her husband out of work. Mrs. Randall sympathized. Her young brother, Wesley Frazier, 19, had come on from Alabama and was also a long time looking for work. He finally got a job at the Texas Book Depository Building.

Mrs. Paine went home and called the building. She got manager Roy Truly and told him that she had a fine young man for him if needed. "Tell him to come on in," Truly replied.

And so it came to be that the last link was in place, put there by an unwitting hand intending only to do good.

* * * *

Every half hour the Honor Guard changed in the East Room. Every two hours new priests came to kneel at the wooden kneeling benches set up before the flag-draped casket. All night long, as the candles burned low in the black wooden holders and the murmur of the crowds outside along Pennsylvania Avenue died to the whispers of a few, the vigil was maintained. The old house that had known such gaiety and grief, that had sheltered every President since John Adams and echoed to Tom Jefferson's violin and Andy Jackson's square dance callers and Abe Lincoln's laughter and Rutherford Hayes' Sunday night hymn singing and Teddy Roosevelt's booming bonhomie, that had glittered with the magic of more than thirty inaugural balls and lowered its lamps to receive the mortal remains of seven of its masters, now stood locked in silence once more.

The marble fireplaces in the East Room were shrouded in black. Franklin Roosevelt's ornate gold piano had been rolled out into the hall. The enormous crystal chandeliers, designed to catch the sparkle of whirling waltzers, now reflected the soft glow of the polished bayonets of the Honor Guard. On the wall behind the coffin, George and Martha Washington looked down from gilt-edged frames. At the head of the coffin stood a large mahogany crucifix, at the foot lay a spray of carnations and lillies, burdening the air with an oppressive fragrance. The only sounds were the occasional sputtering of a candle and the soft turning of prayer book pages.

And in the black moonless night outside, a White House guard moved silently through the foliage, making the rounds as usual.

* * * *

SUNDAY—November 24, 1963

EARLY on Sunday morning, while silent, staring crowds began to gather outside the White House to see the casket carried out the door, Jacqueline Kennedy slipped out to Arlington to inspect the gravesite. In accordance with her wishes, Army engineers had laid it out on a grassy slope below the pillared Custis-Lee Mansion in a direct line with the Lincoln Memorial. Observed only by her Secret Service escort and two grave diggers at work in the trench, she stood for a moment under the bare trees gazing vacantly across the Potomac toward the dome of the Capitol.

Soon the body of her husband would be taken there, up the thirty-six marble steps he had climbed as a young congressman, into the great Rotunda where as a freshman senator he had posed for pictures with the tourists from home, past the very spot where at noontime on a raw January day he had delivered his inaugural address.

All around, the city stretched serene in the sunlight, a pleasant vista of broad lawns and wide boulevards, the granite shaft of the Washington Monument looming over the tile roofed government buildings, the classic columned railroad station lending elegance to the downtown slums, the Victorian tower on the old post office building brooding over the commercial district's cluster of hotels and department stores. After the gloom of yesterday's rain and high winds, the city sparkled again in the way John Kennedy loved to see it when he flew over in his helicopter.

"Nice day for the procession," said a woman behind the ropes in Lafayette Park.

"He'd have loved it," replied the motorcycle cop holding the crowds back.

On other smiling Sundays in Washington, John Kennedy would ride up Pennsylvania Avenue for mid-morning Mass at Sacred Heart Church or go down Connecticut to St. Matthew's Cathedral, just around the corner on Rhode Island.

Today the Rev. Frank Ruppert came out from St. Matthew's to say Mass on a portable altar set up behind the coffin in the East Room. Back from her solitary trip to Arlington, Mrs. Kennedy knelt with her children and other members of the family on the bare floor, listening to the priest intone the ancient Latin prayers. And through the slightly open windows came the faint murmurings of the crowd across the street and tread of marching feet along the circular drive.

Already the parade was forming for the march to the Capitol. A platoon of sailors stood at parade rest in the middle of Pennsylvania Avenue, just outside the White House fence. Behind them, the Joint Chiefs of Staff stood at ease, conversing in whispered tones. Three clergymen, a priest, a rabbi and a minister, took their places in the line of march. One of them, Dean Francis Sayre, Jr. of Washington's National Cathedral,

had been born in the White House. His mother was the daughter of Woodrow Wilson.

Farther up the street, waiting for the starting signal, ten Army drummers began beating out the muffled tattoo that would set the 100-steps-to-the-minute pace of the procession. In the surrounding side streets, units of the Marines, Army, Coast Guard and Air Force lined up to join the procession.

"Look, here comes the caisson!"

Six matched grays, led by a seventh, pulled the black-draped caisson up the White House drive and under the North Portico to await the body of John F. Kennedy. It was the same caisson that had borne the body of Franklin D. Roosevelt.

White House employees, cooks and valets, laundresses and maids, secretaries and guides, gathered forlornly out on the lawn, waiting for their beloved boss to pass down the archway of fifty flags, one for each state, lining the driveway.

It was now 12:20 P.M., Washington time.

All eyes strained toward the black shrouded doorway under the North Portico, watching for the first sight of the casket.

"Hey!" shouted a teen-ager with a transistor radio stuck in his ear, "Oswald was just shot! Listen!"

About the same time, the motorcycle cop holding the crowds back heard it on his radio.

Oswald shot in Dallas! Right in the police station!

The word ran quickly through the crowd and the country, shattering the serenity of that sunlit Sunday.

* * * *

There was nothing much new that morning, but still the people sat by their television sets for any news, for solace, for a feeling that at least this way they could share in the grief of their countrymen.

The emphasis was on religious services and funeral plans. Then the announcer said: "We now switch to Dallas . . ."

It was to be a brief telecast of Oswald being taken from the jail in City Hall to the county jail in the Criminal Courts Building, a move that would cover about thirteen blocks. Oswald would come out of an elevator in the basement and onto a ramp to get into an armored car. Constant viewers since Friday would have recognized the spot by now.

As the elevator slid down from the fourth floor cell block to the basement, detective J. R. Leavelle turned to Oswald.

"If anybody shoots at you, I hope they are as good a shot as you are."

A thin smile crossed the sullen face. "No one is going to shoot at me," the prisoner replied.

*   *   *   *

Earlier that morning, a phone rang in the Dallas FBI office. The caller said Lee Oswald was, indeed, going to be shot. The caller hung up. About 7 A.M. Police Chief Jesse Curry was informed of the call.

The night before, when reporters asked about the transfer,

Curry had told them, "If you fellows are here by 10 A.M., you'll be early enough." And when they showed up at 10, he told them, "We could have done this earlier if I hadn't given you fellows that 10 o'clock time."

Police aren't always that cooperative with the press. But then, the Dallas police had not been overly bashful about the quick arrest and rapid gathering of evidence against Oswald. The prisoner had been carted from room to room during his interrogation in full view of press and camera. Sometimes he almost had to have police in front, running interference. If flashbulbs had been guns, he would have been slain long since.

Yet police weren't letting their guard down. A man was with Oswald at all times in his cell. Officers always surrounded him. They were sure they had the assassin and they didn't want anything to happen to him. For, as District Attorney Henry Wade said, "I have no doubts in this case . . . there is no question he was the killer of President Kennedy." And homicide Capt. Will Fritz said, "I think the case is cinched."

The American Civil Liberties Union later roasted this type of statement as a violation of the first principle of American justice: a man is innocent until proven guilty.

In all the nation, though, only a few, thin voices were heard in defense of Lee Oswald.

—His wife's, in broken English: "I love Lee. Lee good man. He didn't do anything."

—His mother's, with indignation: "If my son had killed the President, he would have said so. That's the way he was brought up."

—His own, as he waved his manacled fists at reporters: "I didn't kill anybody."

—His brother Robert's, calm, judicious: "I will stand by the official report of the case."

Perhaps a number of people would have given a great deal to have just one good shot at Lee Harvey Oswald.

Anyone with such ideas was going to have a time getting into the city jail. Police lines outside the building held back a crowd of two hundred whom a sergeant likened to "a football crowd or a mob ready for a big parade."

An armored car, the kind used to haul money, was backed down the ramp. But a low ceiling prevented it from backing all the way to the doorway from which Oswald would exit. Actually the armored car was a decoy. Oswald would be taken in an unmarked police cruiser.

About 11 A.M. Chief Curry took the newsmen who had crammed into his third floor office down to the basement. Uniformed police checked each reporter's and cameraman's credentials, and FBI agents went through on facial recognition. About fifteen feet across the ramp from the doorway, TV cameras perched on spidery legs. Photographers climbed up on railings, anything, to get a clear view. There were about fifty people present in all.

Behind the door was the booking room, where patrol officers left their arrests. About 11:20 A.M., Capt. Fritz came out. Behind was Oswald.

The prisoner's hands were manacled, his right arm was held by detective Leavelle. Officer L. C. Graves was on Oswald's other side, holding his left arm. Oswald was in black sweater and slacks, his face still marked from the scuffle at his arrest.

74

He also had had a fleeting glimpse of the rifle retreating from the book building window when the President was shot.

Millions of Americans saw the Oswald shooting on TV, live. NBC was televising the scene nationally. ABC and CBS had tapes of the shooting on the air within seconds.

The tragic day had become—what? More tragic? Bewildering? Insane? Everyone had his own reaction. But there was no disputing that the somber dignity of the day had been fouled. And so had the already stained reputation of the nation.

There were those in the land who said "good riddance." This deeply worried many keepers of the American conscience. An eye for an eye and a tooth for a tooth was an ultimate descent into barbarism, they said. But most Americans—and most of Dallas—were stricken at the renewal of brutality. An elderly man outside the Dallas jail threw up his hands in despair. A woman coming from church in New York said: "It's modern anarchy. It's against everything the President stood for."

Radio Moscow, which two days before had reacted to the assassination with genuine grief and spontaneous dignity, returned to its tin trumpet, shrilling that Oswald had been shot down by his co-plotters of the extreme right wing to keep him from talking.

"Jack Ruby political?" snorted Herb Kelly, a former partner of his. "I don't think he ever even voted."

The drama had a few more moments to run.

Parkland Hospital, where Marina Oswald had given birth to her second daughter, where the President had died and Governor Connally was still gravely ill, would be the scene again. An ambulance rushed to the jail to pick up Oswald.

He was unconscious, mouth agape, face ash gray and his head rolled from side to side. When he reached the hospital at 11:32 A.M. and was hurried into Emergency Room Two, the room where Governor Connally had been treated and across the hall from where the President died, there were only occasional death gasps.

By yet another twist of fate, several of the doctors who worked over President Kennedy—including Malcolm Perry—now were treating the man charged with his murder. Whatever their thoughts, theirs, by ancient oath, was to cure, not condemn.

Medically, Oswald had a slightly better chance than the President. His spleen, pancreas, one kidney and liver had been hit and the biggest vein and biggest artery of the body had been damaged. When surgeons cut into his stomach, they found four of the body's eight quarts of blood had poured out of the internal wounds. Yet, after Oswald had been rushed up to surgery, they skillfully stopped the bleeding. "We were very close to saving him," said the 34-year-old Perry.

But ten minutes later, at 12:40 P.M., Oswald's heart stopped. Perry, who had hopelessly massaged President Kennedy's stilled heart, opened Oswald's chest and began doing the same for him. It quivered a few times but at 1:03 there was no beat and at 1:07 Lee Harvey Oswald was pronounced dead. It was two days and seven minutes after some of the same doctors had pronounced the same verdict over the body of the President of the United States.

* * * *

One of the reporters was Francois Pelou, a Frenchman: "Oswald was squinting a little because of the bright lights but he came out very calmly and he had this faint smile on his face. Then this man in a brown suit and hat—he was sort of crouching—rushed up to him."

FLASH
DALLAS (AP)—OSWALD SHOT.

Officer B. H. Combest also saw the blur of the man coming. "He was bootlegging the pistol like a quarterback with a football and he just brought it up and fired."

Combest recognized the man.

"I knew what he was going to do. I shouted, 'Jack, you son of a bitch,' but I couldn't get at him."

The man he recognized was Jack Ruby, a 52-year-old operator of sleazy nightclubs who was often around headquarters. He was a fringe friend of the force, a nervous, pushy man who stoked the furnace of his ego with boasts of how close he always was to "the inside."

Ruby fired only once. Almost simultaneous with the shot from his .38 caliber, snub-nosed revolver came a high, animal scream from Oswald. He blinked his eyes and crossed his arms protectively over his middle. But it was too late. The slug had struck home, an inch below the heart. Oswald toppled. And, just an hour less than two days after John Kennedy was shot down, bedlam broke out again in Dallas.

Some officers hastily dragged Oswald back through the door and soon became jammed up in the doorway. Others jumped Jack Ruby and quickly subdued and disarmed him. In the confusion, reporters scampered behind pillars.

Bob Jackson, photographer for the Dallas Times Herald, got a classic picture of the very moment the bullet hit Oswald.

Marina Oswald had been taken to the home of Irving Police Chief C. J. Wirasnik for her own protection and was watching the news of her husband's shooting on television. Her baby, Audrey, slept on the couch beside her. Her other child, June, played with a borrowed doll on the floor. Her mother-in-law was outside in a patrol car listening to the police radio and got the news first.

"Now it's all over with," she cried, running into the house.

"I want to see him, I want to see him!" sobbed Marina in English. The baby woke. The mother fed her briefly and then the women, with the children, sped to the hospital.

Back at police headquarters, Jack Ruby was charged with murder and jailed. Outside Capt. Fritz's office newsmen crowded around Ruby with the same question they had thrown at Oswald: "Why did you do it?"

Jack Ruby blinked at them in astonishment, perhaps at their naiveté. But he said nothing.

* * * *

Mrs. Livingston, Lee Oswald's fourth grade teacher, said after he was shot: "He wasn't for anything. He wasn't against anything. He just *wasn't* anything."

But he was. In the end he was called a killer. And around the refuse of his muddled life questions buzzed like flies.

Why did he do it? Did something, some little something, finally blow open the locks that clamped his buried hate? Was he the clumsy agent of a secret plot? Police investigated whether he had been the man who shot at and just missed Maj. Gen. Edwin Walker in Dallas the previous spring. Did those letters found in his apartment bearing Communist letterheads and talking about organizing Fair Play for Cuba committees indicate Oswald was not acting alone? The FBI very much doubted it.

Was his act the capstone of a long campaign of vile stealth? Who knows, but he didn't seek out a job at the book building. Mrs. Paine did. And it was only chance that he wasn't working several blocks away. Was he suddenly maddened and beyond reality? Did that gloomy, hypnotic idol of Karl Marx drive him? Mrs. Paine's husband, Michael, said that Oswald clung against all argument to Marxist doctrine without really understanding it and predicted that it, either violently or not, would someday inherit the earth.

Or was it a deeper demon whose nature we can only guess? Surely there was enough to make the pensive psychiatrist nod his head sagely: the boy's wandering, fatherless, friendless childhood; his thirsty absorption of a shattering creed that offered promise to a life that had little; the dreary reality that rusted this promise away.

Does such analysis explain the impossible, infuriating contradictions of Lee Oswald: a man who talked of a more perfect society and skipped out on his rent in this one; a man who believed in communal action of the masses but who lost every friend he ever had; a man deprived by fate and given to tyrannizing his wife; a man who came home to help his ailing mother but who left her three days later with $1,000 in his pocket; a man who fled his homeland in disgust and then indignantly demanded he be allowed to return; a nobody who argued against all evidence that he was a somebody.

Most likely all of this is explainable—and related. But when the jigsaw pieces are all fitted together, there is still no picture. When the figures are all added up, there is still no total.

We still do not know why the President was shot.

For, if John F. Kennedy belongs to the ages, so, too, does Lee Harvey Oswald.

* * * *

Tum—Tum—Tum. R-o-o-o-o-o-o-o-ll.
Tum—Tum—Tum. R-o-o-o-o-o-o-o-ll.

Down Pennsylvania Avenue from the White House to the Capitol the funeral cortege flowed, retracing in sad reversal the path John Kennedy had traveled in his triumphant inaugural parade.

Down Pennsylvania Avenue it flowed, to the mournful beat of the muffled drums and the slow clip-clop of the seven matched grays pulling the high-wheeled caisson, to the skittish gait of the black riderless horse with the polished cavalry boots reversed in the stirrups and the silver sword dangling from an empty saddle.

Down Pennsylvania Avenue in streaming sunlight it flowed, at a pace of one hundred steps to the minute, through the canyons of mute staring faces, past the teen-agers clinging to statues and perched in the trees like starlings, past the grim gray government buildings with the flags at half staff and the doorways draped in black.

Down Pennsylvania Avenue on a sad Sunday afternoon it flowed, with the beautiful young widow staring straight ahead under a black lace mantilla in the back seat of the black limousine, and Caroline and little John pressing their noses against the back window, and the new President of the United States and the new First Lady riding in the jump seats.

Down Pennsylvania Avenue it flowed, with the Joint Chiefs of Staff marching straight and tall, and a lone sailor proudly holding aloft the presidential flag, and the White House press shambling along behind, and the crowd streaming off the sidewalk trying to join in the procession.

Down Pennsylvania and onto Constitution and onto the Capitol grounds it flowed, with the transistor radios just then crackling out the word that Lee Harvey Oswald was dead, too.

"Good enough for him," they wanted to say, and some even did say, but no universal cry of revenge diluted the grief along the stricken street.

John F. Kennedy was being carried to lie in state in the great Rotunda of the Capitol, on the same catafalque that had cradled Abraham Lincoln. Nothing could detract from the solemnity of that scene. Vengeance died in the throat, smothered by the mournful echo of the muffled drums. To those along the street, primitive violence in Dallas seemed a world away.

Nine pall bearers, representing all branches of the armed forces, carried the heavy mahogany casket up the thirty-six steps of the Capitol, as a chorus of midshipmen softly intoned the Navy Hymn.

Eyes fixed straight ahead on the casket, Mrs. Kennedy followed them up the stairs, leading Caroline and John by the hand. They took their places behind the velvet ropes separating the casket and honor guard from the dignitaries, the senators and representatives, the cabinet members and Supreme Court justices, foreign diplomats and White House staff members, who crowded round in the great chamber.

"And so she took the ring from her finger and placed it in his hand . . ."

Five times Sen. Mike Mansfield repeated the line, so cruelly specific, in his choked eulogy. The widow seemed to sway a bit, but her face never lost its look of grief in stone.

Chief Justice Earl Warren's eulogy was less personal and more pointed: "If we really love this country, if we truly love justice and mercy, if we fervently want to make this nation better for those who are to follow us, we can at least abjure the hatred that consumes people, the false accusations that divide us and the bitterness that begets violence."

Tears ran down Robert Kennedy's face as House Speaker

John McCormack centered his eulogy on the virtues of the deceased: "He had the bravery and a sense of personal duty which made him willing to face up to the great task of being President in these trying times. He had the warmth and the sense of humanity which made the burden of the task bearable for himself and his associates and which made all kinds of diverse peoples and races eager to be associated with him in his task."

Caroline stood straight and unmoving during the long ceremony, but little John began to fidget, pulling at his mother's coat, gazing at the ceiling and then visiting noisily among the soldiers and dignitaries. A nurse took him out to the Speaker's office, where he spotted a small American flag on the desk.

"I want to take that home to my Daddy," he said to the receptionist.

Later, when he reappeared in the Rotunda, he was clutching the little flag in his white-gloved hand.

After the eulogies, Jacqueline Kennedy led Caroline toward the casket. "Kneel down," she said softly. And then she kissed the coffin, reverently, lovingly, while Caroline groped beneath the flag to touch the hard shiny wood.

President Johnson came forward to pay his respects, preceded by a soldier walking backward carrying a huge wreath of red and white carnations with the inscription, "From President Johnson and the Nation." Then the various dignitaries began to file by, each pausing for a second with bowed head before the casket.

Outside, the crowd, on its own, had formed itself into a long line to pass into the Rotunda and view the bier. The day had suddenly turned cold, as the sun died in a pinkish glow behind the Capitol dome, but the line grew longer and longer. Within a half hour, it stretched twenty blocks, a silent, shivering stream of mourners which by dawn would grow to a great river of sorrow.

* * * *

81

Jack Ruby was forever on the fringes, never quite getting inside. And Jack Ruby ends up in history as a bizarre footnote on a tragic page.

When Gene Tunney beat Jack Dempsey in Chicago on September 22, 1927, Jack Ruby was there, briefly. He crashed the gate and somebody found out and he was thrown out. He liked to drop names, Jack did, the names of big time hoodlums. But if you asked the hoods about Jack Ruby they'd look blank and wonder who you were talking about.

Jack Ruby was difficult to figure.

If he liked you and he had $300 in his pocket and you were broke, he might give you half. He was like that. But if he didn't like you, people said, he might smash you in the face with a pudgy fist and throw you down the stairs. He was like that, too.

Generosity to friends, brutality to enemies, that was part of growing up on the tough Chicago West Side where he was born Jack Leon Rubenstein on March 25, 1911, one of eight children of Orthodox Jewish immigrants from Poland. Much

later, he had his name changed legally to Ruby.

In spite of his reputation as a street brawler, people thought of him as quite religious. He didn't drink; he didn't smoke; he rarely used profanity. A bachelor, he wanted to be thought of as gallant with women, even though he once threatened to beat up a dancer and burn her wardrobe in an argument over money.

He spent most of his first forty years in Chicago, selling things like cigars, janitor supplies, novelties, auto accessories, even little statues of Gen. Douglas MacArthur, for he was a patriotic man, Jack Ruby was. He also scalped theater and sports tickets and gambled steadily in a small way.

For a brief time, he boxed under the name of "Sparkling Ruby" and the nickname stuck as "Sparky." He did considerable fighting outside the ring, too. He was ready to swing at the drop of a crack about President Franklin D. Roosevelt. He loved FDR. "He loved every President," said his sister, Mrs. Eva Grant of Dallas. "That's the whole problem."

Ruby came to Dallas in 1948 to run a night club for his

sister. In those early days in Big D, he affected western dress and the people who knew him called him wryly "the Chicago cowboy." Later, his taste in clothing shifted back to big time operator styles with the snap brim hat worn low over his eyes, like Al Capone.

By November, 1963, Ruby owned two clubs in Dallas, the Carousel, a downtown strip tease joint, and the Vegas, a rock 'n' roll dance hall in the Oaklawn section. He was good for about $15,000 a year and he shared an apartment, with a swimming pool, in the Oak Cliff section with George Senator, who sometimes worked for him. Jack Ruby never had it so good.

But he was still hanging around. A stocky, balding, fast-talking man, a kibitzer on the fringes.

He boasted that he knew every policeman in Dallas and every reporter, too. He had a minor police record, including two arrests for carrying concealed weapons. He had a lot of money with him at times and, he said, he carried the nickel-plated .38 caliber pistol just for protection.

Shortly after noon, on Friday, November 22, Jack Ruby sat in the advertising department of the Dallas Morning News consulting with John Newnam about the layout of his ads for the Carousel and the Vegas. Suddenly a man burst into the room and shouted: "The President's been shot!" Ruby's mouth sagged open in disbelief. So far, his reaction was no different from anyone else's.

For the next hour or so, he watched television with Newnam. With each new development in the burgeoning tragedy, Ruby grew increasingly more depressed. He admired Jack Kennedy. The President had class and a large part of Jack Ruby's life was devoted to a search for class. He never made it.

He cancelled his ads. It was the class thing to do. He went down to the Carousel and scrawled "CLOSED" across the door. He called his sister. Mrs. Grant thought he was more upset about the President's death than he was over the death of their 88-year-old father five years before. He called his brother, Earle, in Detroit and, over the telephone, he cried.

Friday evening he followed a strange sequence. He called Don Safran, amusements columnist of the Dallas Times Herald, to announce that he was closing his clubs. It was the classy thing to do and why keep it a secret?

"Who can think of business at a time like this?" he said. "I bawled like a baby when I first heard the news. I'm sick. I haven't been able to think. I loved that man."

Moments later, he was on the line to Safran again.

"I don't know when I'll reopen," he said. "My family is taking this badly."

He called Safran a third time.

"Don," he said, "you aren't going to call the other clubs, are you, and tell them I'm closed. I don't think they ought to be forced into closing just because I am. It's their decision. Let them worry about their own ideals."

Safran thought he sounded more and more agitated. But, then, wasn't everybody?

Saturday was an aimless day for Jack Ruby. He watched television, sometimes at home, sometimes with his sister. He called Mrs. Grant at least six times. "He (Kennedy) could have been anything," he told her once. "Anything he wanted to be. Anything in life. And he had to end up this way."

He paced the floor of his apartment and told George Senator over and over: "Those poor kids. Those poor kids."

He was watching television with his sister when he saw Oswald. They agreed that the accused assassin looked like a "creep." Through the electronic tube he hated Oswald with such a passion that Mrs. Grant felt she had to comfort him.

"Don't worry," she said. "Someone will get Oswald."

Jack Ruby disagreed.

"Look at the logic of this," he said. "Oswald got the President but no one can get to Oswald."

Saturday night he brought sandwiches and coffee to the policemen and newsmen at City Hall. He was still hanging around. He even sat in on a news conference called by Police Chief Jesse Curry. Someone asked him what he was doing there. Wasn't the news conference just for newsmen?

"Oh, I know all the policemen and the newsmen," said Jack Ruby airily. "I just came down to listen in."

He saw Oswald face to face and he despised him even more because "he was so smirky; he was so smart, acted so proud of what he had done."

Nevertheless, mourning Jack Ruby took the time to pass out Carousel Club cards to out-of-town newsmen. The cards had a line drawing of a nude girl in black net stockings and black gloves and a glass of bubbling champagne. The rising bubbles were labeled "GIRLS! GIRLS! GIRLS!" and the cards

identified "Your host, Jack Ruby." That was Jack Ruby, class all the way.

He was up earlier than usual on Sunday morning and took his daily dip in the apartment house pool. He wore a bathing cap because he was afraid of losing his hair. He picked up Sheba, one of his three dachshunds, and told Senator he was going downtown. He also picked up his nickel-plated .38.

For the fourth or fifth time since Friday, he wandered back to the assassination scene. Soon, he planned to bring flowers and strew them by the roadside. He drove to the Western Union office on Main Street and sent a $25 money order to one of his strippers who lived in Fort Worth and was behind in her room rent. More important, Jack Ruby was now only a few steps from City Hall. The sun-washed four-story building drew him like a magnet. It was 11:16 A.M.

He walked down Main and paused before the entrance to the underground garage. A single policeman stood watch. A squad car rolled up the ramp and stopped. The policeman on watch went over to talk to the man in the car. Unnoticed, Jack Ruby, free lance avenger, walked past them and down the ramp into the basement of the building.

* * * *

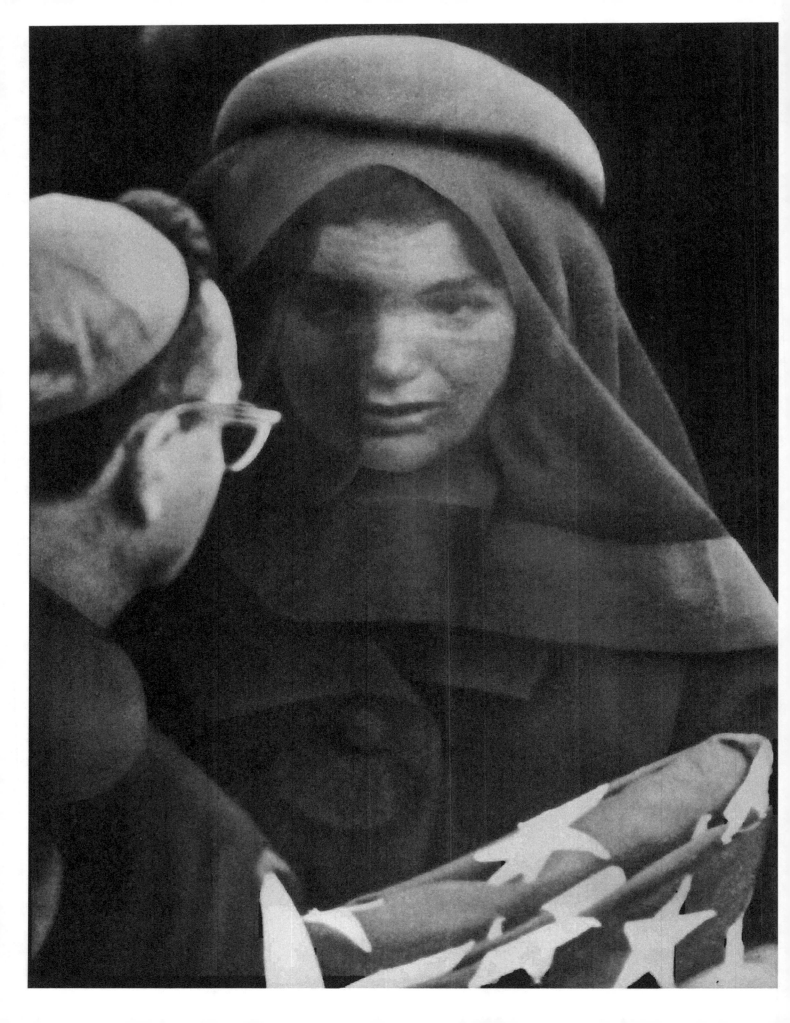

They had planned to close the great gold doors of the Rotunda at 9 P.M., but by then the line stretched for nearly two miles into the chill night. And still it grew. Eight abreast, snaking across the Capitol grounds and up Constitution Avenue as far as the eye could see, the mourners stood in shivering silence, waiting to file past the flag-draped coffin. All night long they shuffled through the Rotunda in two separate lines, flowing in a great slow circle which the guards kept moving with hushed admonitions.

Two teen-agers had walked forty miles from Baltimore to join the line. A convent of thirty-six nuns from Jersey City chartered a bus to come to the capital and pray at the bier. They moved past the casket shortly before midnight, saying their beads half aloud in a murmuring sing-song. At 2:30 A.M., former heavyweight champion Jersey Joe Walcott went by. He had waited in line for nearly eight hours.

By dawn, guards were telling mourners at the tail end of the line that there was no hope of getting in, but still they kept coming.

During the night, Jacqueline Kennedy returned to the Rotunda with Bobby Kennedy. She slipped through the line of mourners, past the red velvet ropes, and knelt at the coffin. Again, she leaned forward and kissed the flag. Before leaving, she looked for a long time into the faces of the silent mourners, as if trying to rivet their sorrowing expressions for-ever in her mind. For a brief moment, a thin, grateful smile parted her lips.

Outside in the raw night air, she said to Bobby Kennedy, "Let's walk a bit."

Two ghostly figures in the faint light of the ornate Capitol lamps, they moved down the lawn and along the waiting line. On the Senate side of the Capitol, they went down the hill and crossed the street to a waiting limousine that had followed them at a respectful distance. Before getting in, Jackie turned back to gaze once more at the floodlit Capitol dome and the numb, silent throng flowing up the great marble staircase out of the night.

By mid-morning, when the great gold doors finally swung shut, more than a quarter of a million people had filed by.

And so this incredible Sunday ended, a sunlit day of sad splendor streaked with the ugly shadow of violent revenge, a day of grief turned suddenly grotesque. A man named Jack Ruby had moved out of the crowd to commit an uncivilized act in behalf of a highly civilized man.

"My God, my God! What are we coming to?"

The anguished words of Speaker McCormack seemed to hang in the air like the doomsday echo of the drums.

* * * *

MONDAY—November 25, 1963

THE SILVER-GRAY casket of policeman J. D. Tippitt was lowered into its final resting place in a section of Laurel Land Memorial Park set aside for those who gave their lives in the service of Dallas.

Four hundred people crowded into Beckley Hills Baptist Church and a thousand more stood outside as the Rev. C. D. Tipps, Jr. eulogized the dead hero: "He was doing his duty when he was taken from us by a poor, confused, misguided assassin, as was the President of the United States."

The widow, Marie Tippitt, had received telephoned messages of sympathy from President Johnson and Attorney General Robert Kennedy. Now she stood for a long, wordless moment before the casket. Then, with her handkerchief to her eyes, she turned away and she was heard to whisper: "God, oh God."

* * * *

Forty minutes later and thirty miles away, a large crowd gathered for the funeral of Lee Harvey Oswald in Fort Worth but only five could be called mourners and two of them really didn't understand.

The Secret Service had arranged for the burial and tried to keep it secret. But forty newsmen heard about it and there were a hundred Fort Worth policemen on hand to protect the mourners and the body. A few curious craned their necks behind a stone wall to watch the ceremony in an isolated section of Rose Hill Cemetery.

The body of Oswald was taken to the cemetery in a heavily guarded hearse and kept in a small chapel until the family arrived. The requested minister didn't appear. At the last moment, the Rev. Louis Saunders, executive secretary of the Fort Worth Council of Churches, volunteered to officiate.

"We are not here to judge; we are here to lay him away before an understanding God," he said gently over the body of Lee Harvey Oswald, atheist. There was no mention of the assassination.

The lid of the plain, mole-skin covered wooden coffin was raised for a moment and Mrs. Marina Oswald looked down at her husband for the last time. She held her daughter June, 22 months old, in her arms and she told the uncomprehending child in halting English: "Look, Daddy sleeps."

Then, weeping, she kissed him and slipped the wedding ring from her hand and placed it on his finger.

The lid was closed and the coffin was lowered into the ground as the mourners—Marina holding June; Mrs. Marguerite Oswald holding Audrey, five weeks old; and brother Robert—sprinkled handfuls of dirt into the trench. Then they were spirited away to a secret hiding place by the Secret Service.

Two grave diggers remained. They had been told they were digging the grave for a man named William Bobo but now they shoveled dirt over the mortal remains of Lee Harvey Oswald and all his secrets.

* * * *

The sun was bright and the sky clear and blue and the presidents and the prime ministers and the king and the princes were ready, the whole panoply of power and grandeur, foreign and domestic, was ready. Under the handsome hanging lantern of the North Portico, the caisson and the coffin under the flag were ready. He was leaving the noble old house for the last time and one tried to remember what drew John Kennedy here the first time. It was, he used to say, the center of action and the center of action always pulled at him, at home or at college, at war or at peace. And so he went into politics, this man who was not a natural politician, this man whose sense of privacy and dignity rebelled at the Indian feathers to be worn and the babies to be kissed and the whole turning outside of the inside of a man. But there was the center of action pulling at him and there was his favorite proverb from the Greeks, "Happiness is the full use of your powers along lines of excellence in a life affording scope." Here, at this old house, had he reached the peak of his happiness and the peak of his powers?...

But now it was time to go.

The muffled drums began and the cadets of the academies moved forward, and across the way, through the elms and over the lawn, the bells of old St. John's Episcopal, "the Church of Presidents," began to toll. And the Black Watch bagpipers moved into place, as so many small parts moved into place, because Jacqueline Kennedy had remembered, as she remembered so much for this day, that two weeks ago on the White House lawn he had enjoyed their music. There came then striding up the avenue the Joint Chiefs of Staff, heroic in braid, the symbols of the vast power that could not save him. Could not save the man who had survived the war as a Navy lieu-

tenant but not the peace as commander-in-chief. There came then the seven matched grays pulling the caisson and casket and the riderless horse, empty boots reversed, silver sword sheathed, in the ancient manner of mourning the fallen warrior.

There came then Jacqueline Kennedy, now the pride of a nation, and she suddenly let go the hand of Robert Kennedy and, as if from some deep inner resolution, stepped out on her own, head high, shoulders back, stride firm. Up the avenue she strode, beautiful in black and gallant in purpose, with her husband's brothers and sisters and their wives and their husbands, this remarkable family whose number included a President and a member of the Cabinet and a member of the Senate of the United States.

There came then the new President and the new First Lady, surrounded by young men nervously scanning the huge muted crowd along the curb and the windows above and the rooftops above them, and all sudden movement near and far.

There came then the strangest of all sights, in large shapes and small, in cadence and out, the princes and kings, the foreign presidents and prime ministers, marching up an American street past American drugstores and American cafeterias and Americans mourning an American President. De Gaulle of France in olive gray, Selassie of Ethiopia heavy with medals, Baudouin of Belgium in khaki, Philip of England in Royal Navy blue, Frederika of Greece in a fur coat, Mikoyan of Russia in black coat and striped trousers; in all two hundred and twenty marching symbols from ninety-two nations.

There came then, from the government, from the government of law, the Justices of the Supreme Court and the men of the Cabinet and the men of the Congress and, perhaps saddest of all, the tiny group of close friends and advisors who had followed him all the way and were still following him; Pierre Salinger, who worried about his image and Ted Sorenson, about his rhetoric, and Kenny O'Donnell, about his appointments and much more than that.

At the steps of the cathedral, St. Matthew's Cathedral, the caisson stopped and the uniformed pallbearers began gently to remove the casket. Inside the church, Richard Cardinal Cushing of Boston, in tall mitre and black vestments, walked down the aisle and near the door met a veiled woman in black.

"Rose, my dear, my dear," he said, embracing the mother of the dead President.

And the old Cardinal walked down the steps and out into the street to receive the body. Jacqueline Kennedy, now joined by her children, knelt to kiss his ring and the craggy-faced old Cardinal leaned down to kiss Caroline and pat little John, who had begun to cry on this, his third birthday. And so he was still there, in the march of the family milestones, the same gaunt old priest, who had married John and Jacqueline Kennedy ten years ago and baptized their children and presided at the funeral of their infant son and droned out the invocation at the inaugural of the 35th President of the United States.

And into the cathedral they all went, the living and the dead, the old Cardinal and the family, the princes and presidents, gathered under the great green dome of the church in such diversity as to include Dwight Eisenhower and Harry Truman and John Glenn and Richard Nixon and Nelson Rockefeller and Barry Goldwater and Billy Graham and Henry Ford II and George Wallace of Alabama and Martin Luther King of Georgia. And the old Cardinal began, in Latin, the opening prayers of the simple low requiem Mass, while Luigi Vena, a tenor, rose in the choir loft to sing "Ave Maria," just as he did when John and Jacqueline Kennedy were married in Newport a decade ago. The ceremony moved on, and little John, because he was getting bored, was taken out and given a pamphlet from the rack in the vestibule to occupy his wandering attention.

And at the end of the Mass, with a sprinkler of holy water in his hand, the old Cardinal circled the coffin, blessing it as he went. "May the angels, dear Jack, lead you into Paradise," he intoned in English. "May the martyrs receive you at your coming. May the spirit of God embrace you, and mayest thou, with all those who made the supreme sacrifice of dying for others, receive eternal rest and peace. Amen."

And the Most Rev. Philip M. Hannan, Auxiliary Bishop of Washington, mounted the pulpit and began his eulogy with one of John Kennedy's favorite passages, from the third chapter of Ecclesiastes: "There is an appointed time for everything ...a time to be born and a time to die...a time to love and a time to hate...a time of war and a time of peace...."

And the priest in the pulpit closed with a long passage from John Kennedy's inaugural address and once more there returned the vision of a new young leader, the vapors of his breath circling his head in the wintry air, calling his countrymen to a new journey....

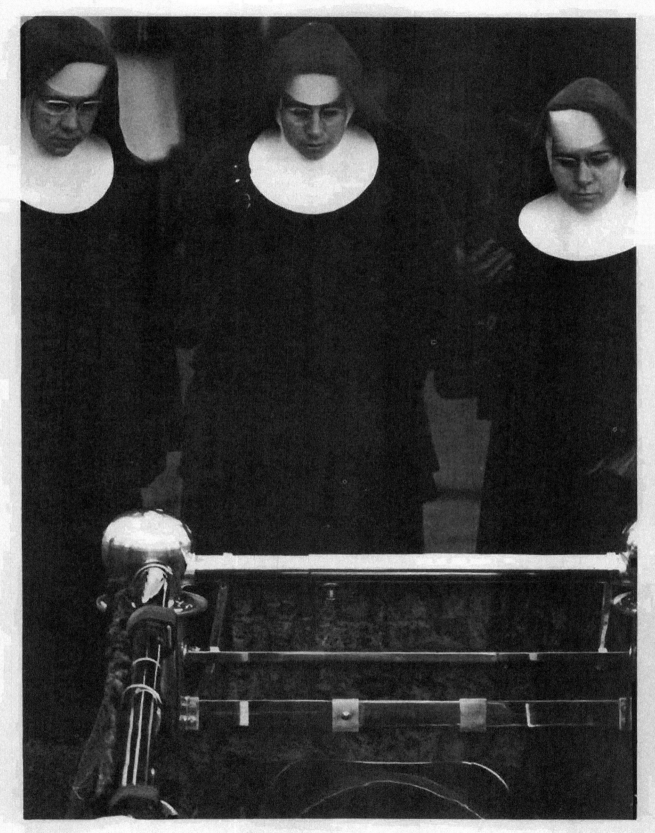

"... Let the word go forth from this time and place, to friend and foe alike, that the torch has been passed to a new generation of Americans—born in this century, tempered by war, disciplined by a hard and bitter peace, proud of their ancient heritage—and unwilling to witness or permit the slow undoing of those human rights to which this nation has always been committed, and to which we are committed today at home and around the world.

"Let every nation know, whether it wishes us well or ill, that we shall pay any price, bear any burden, meet any hardship, support any friend, oppose any foe to assure the survival and the success of liberty.

"Let both sides unite to heed in all corners of the earth the command of Isaiah—'to undo the heavy burdens ... and let the oppressed go free.'

"All this will not be finished in the first hundred days, nor will it be finished in the first thousand days, nor in the life of this administration, nor even, perhaps, in our lifetime on this planet.

"But let us begin...."

And now two years and ten months later, in death not in life, it was time to move again. And once more they carried the casket out into the bright sunlight and Jacqueline Kennedy paused momentarily on the steps of the church with her children at her side. As he watched his father's casket being borne down the steps, little John Kennedy squinted in the sun and saluted.

And the procession reformed, this time in cars, and rolled slowly down the broad boulevard, past the Lincoln Memorial, over the Memorial Bridge and through the high iron gates of the Arlington National Cemetery, and the line was so long

that the last cars were still leaving the cathedral as the first cars were entering the cemetery three miles away. The bagpipers of the Air Force marched through the gates and disappeared over the lip of the hill, playing "The Mist Covered the Mountain," one of John Kennedy's favorite tunes. And the Marine Corps Band played "The Star Spangled Banner" as the body was carried up the grassy slope, the same slope John Kennedy had visited on a smiling spring day last March. "I could stay up here forever," he had said then.

Forever was here and the sun was sinking behind the Virginia hills as the wife and the mother and the brothers and the sisters of the dead President took their places around the grave. For a moment Jacqueline Kennedy seemed uncertain and started blindly toward the grave, but then she was guided gently to her seat by Robert Kennedy.

The old Cardinal came forward again and, in a monotonous flow timed to the eternal rhythm of death, in a tone pitched to the spheres, he commended the body of "this wonderful man, Jack Kennedy," to God. From out of the sky in the south fifty jets roared overhead and there again was Air Force One now dipping its wings, now again as majestic as the "United States of America" lettered along its length. And three cannons, firing in turn, pounded out the last 21-gun salute and up on the hill three riflemen fired a final farewell volley of three rounds.

Taps was sounded over the hill and the flag was raised taut and level over the coffin and folded with loving care and passed from hand to hand to the hand of the widow and the eternal flame was lighted and the Lord's Prayer was intoned once more. And at 3:34 o'clock, on the afternoon of the fourth day, John Fitzgerald Kennedy slipped out of mortal sight—out of sight but not out of heart and mind.

"...and crown thy good with brotherhood..."

ACKNOWLEDGMENT

This book grew out of the work of many Associated Press men and women both on our staff and on our members' staffs who were on the streets of Dallas and Washington to report the four days in November which numbed a nation and a world.

In the 115 years that The Associated Press has gathered news around the world, nothing short of a war has required such instantaneous marshalling of people and resources by this cooperative press association. The torrent of events from that black Friday in Dallas to the sounding of taps at Arlington moved the nation through the entire emotional spectrum. While a nation could be halted, dazed and inert with grief and horror—the newsman could not.

The story required the best from The Associated Press writers, photographers and membership around the world to tell and show this incredible drama which combined murder and majesty.

The effort was not confined to newsmen in Dallas and Washington but spread to Paris, Moscow, Saigon and Tokyo and a hundred other spots which reported the reaction of a stunned world.

We are proud to present a story of this cooperative effort for historians of the future. All of the material in this book came from the AP staff and members except for two portraits by Karsh. In the interest of easy reading, it was put together into one cohesive story by a special team of writers who are listed below.

My thanks to this team and to all The Associated Press men who participated and to the members who contributed. Because of the magnitude of the story, it is possible that we have overlooked some in the credits listed below, and to them my apologies.

Wes Gallagher

WES GALLAGHER
General Manager

"The Torch Is Passed" was written by Saul Pett, Sid Moody, Hugh Mulligan and Tom Henshaw

Supervising Editor—Keith Fuller

The following Associated Press writers, editors, photographers and technicians worked on the original AP coverage of the fateful events in Dallas and Washington Listed also are The Associated Press newspaper and broadcast members who assisted the AP in addition to their own original coverage.

WASHINGTON
William Beale, Jr.,
 Chief of Bureau
William Arbogast
Marvin Arrowsmith
Robert Baer
Jerry Baulch
Karl Bauman
John Beckler
Jack Bell
Gardner Bridge
R Gordon Brown
Francis Carey
James Cary
Anthony Catella
John Chadwick
Martha Cole
Adren Cooper
Francis Cormier
Douglas Cornell
Joseph Coyne
Raymond Crowley
James Davis
Spencer Davis
Louis Easley
Arthur Edson
Jacob Engle
Hamilton Faron
Elton Fay
Belmont Foster
Henry Garrett

Robert Geiger
Neil Gilbride
Geoffrey Gould
Dillon Graham
Sterling Green
Merle Gulick
Edwin Haakinson
Joseph Hall
Charles Haslet
Vernon Haugland
Lewis Hawkins
Edward Higgs
John Hightower
Gaylord Hodenfield
Fred Hoffman
Harrison Humphries
Robert Hunt
Joseph Jamieson
Louis Johrden
John Kamps
Joseph Kane
G. Milton Kelly
Margaret Kernodle De Chard
John Koenig
Edmond LeBreton
Frances Lewine
C. Yates McDaniel
Walker MacFarlan
James Marlow
Ovid Martin

Endre Marton
Walter Mears
Stanley Meisler
Ben Meyer
W. H. Mobley
Joseph Mohbat
James Munn
Larry Osius
Robert Otey
William Owen
William Peacock
Richard Powers
Bem Price
Warner Ragsdale
Arthur Roberts
Donald Sanders
Barry Schweid
Robert Stevenson
Frank Taylor
J Frank Tragle
Ernest Vaccaro
Alfred Wall
Ralph Wallis
Ernest Warren
Bennett Wolfe
Paul Yost
Harry J Kelly
John Barbour
Carl Leubsdorf
Aristides Moleon
William Allen

Henry Burroughs
Harvey Georges
Charles Gorry
Henry Griffin
Byron Rollins
John Rous
Robert Schutz
William Smith

DALLAS
Robert H Johnson, Jr.,
 Texas chief of bureau
J. M Edwards
James W. Mangan
Robert E Ford
Charles H. Green
Mike Cochran
Arno C Adams
Marvin Brau
Marshall Comerer
Clayton E Hickerson
Richard McMurray
Finis Mothershead
Harold V Ratliff
Peggy Simpson
Patricia Curran
Jerry Pillard
Jack Keever
David Taylor
Ferd Kaufman
Carl E Linde

Ted Powers
Joan Jones
James W Altgens
Harold Waters
Robert A. Jarboe

PHILADELPHIA
Bill Achatz
Bill Ingraham

BOSTON:
 (Hyannis Port)
Francis Curtin
William Chaplis
J Walter Green
Cornelius F Hurley
Arthur Ristau

OKLAHOMA CITY·
Wilbur Martin,
 *Oklahoma
 chief of bureau*

NEW YORK
Pat McDonald
Bob Tieken
Bill Gibson
Eddie Adams
Harry Harris
John Rooney
Tom Cottrell
Sol Horn
Woodrow Emanuel
Marty Mauro
Saul Pett
Bernard Gavzer

Arthur Everett
Jules Loh
Hugh Mulligan
Sid Moody

LOS ANGELES
Richard Strobel
Mike Smith

BALTIMORE:
Bill Smith
Jack Blevins

RALEIGH
Perry Aycock

PARIS, FRANCE·
Richard K. O'Malley

MEMBERS
The Dallas Morning News
The Dallas Times Herald
CBS-TV
NBC-TV
ABC-TV
The Washington Star
The Washington Post
The New York Daily News

AP Production by Edward T. Fleming
Printed in U S A by Western Printing & Lithographing Co
Designed by Edward P. Diehl

ILLUSTRATIONS

Page 2—President Kennedy's bier rests in the Capitol Rotunda before a statue of Lincoln.

Pages 4-5—President and Mrs. Kennedy at Love Field.

Page 6, top—President and Mrs. Kennedy arrive at Love Field

Page 6, bottom—The President greets admirers at Love Field

Page 8—Mrs Kennedy with the bouquet of roses presented to her at Love Field.

Pages 10-11—President and Mrs. Kennedy, accompanied by Gov. Connally, leave Love Field.

Page 13—The presidential party, on Houston St. in Dallas, a minute before President Kennedy was slain.

Page 16-17—A photo sequence at the moment of the assassination.

Page 18—U.S. District Judge Sarah T Hughes administers the oath to President Lyndon B Johnson aboard Air Force One.

Page 19—President and Mrs. Johnson console Mrs. Kennedy.

Page 20—Mrs. Kennedy, blood splattered, enters the ambulance with her husband's coffin on arrival at Andrews.

Page 21—The catafalque, in the East Room of the White House

Page 22—Former President Harry S Truman arrives at the White House, escorted by R. Sargent Shriver.

Page 23—Former President Dwight D. Eisenhower arrives at the White House.

Pages 24-25—The honor guard stands vigil and a priest prays before the bier in the East Room of the White House

Pages 26-27—Artillery at Ft. Myer, Va., booms a salute at dawn Saturday.

Page 28—Mrs. Kennedy and her children, and Attorney General Robert Kennedy and his sister, Mrs. Stephen Smith, leave the White House.

Page 29—Mrs. Kennedy and her children follow the coffin down the steps of the White House.

Pages 30-31—The horse-drawn caisson bearing the President's coffin leaves the White House.

Page 32—The cortege moves down Pennsylvania Ave. from the White House toward the Capitol

Page 33—The caisson at the Capitol steps

Pages 34-35—The coffin is borne up the Capitol steps.

Page 36—President Johnson places a wreath at the bier.

Page 37—A view of the catafalque from the Capitol dome.

Pages 38-39—Her daughter at her side, Mrs. Kennedy kisses her husband's coffin as it lies in state at the Capitol.

Page 41—John Fitzgerald Kennedy. (Photo by Karsh, Ottawa)

Page 42—Mrs. John F. Kennedy. (Photo by Karsh, Ottawa)

Page 43—The President's coffin arrives at the Capitol.

Page 44—President Kennedy's grave.

Page 45—Mrs Jacqueline Kennedy.

Pages 46-47, top—Senate Majority Leader Mansfield, third from left, wearing dark-rimmed glasses, delivers a eulogy at the Capitol Rotunda.

Page 46, bottom—President Johnson and members of the Kennedy family listen as Chief Justice Earl Warren delivers a eulogy in the Capitol Rotunda.

Page 48—The President's widow and children and members of his family descend the Capitol steps.

Page 49—The President and Mrs. Johnson, Mrs. Kennedy and her son, John, Jr., and Attorney General Robert Kennedy leave the Capitol.

Page 50—Mrs. Kennedy and Attorney General Robert Kennedy.

Pages 51 to 54—Americans pay homage to their fallen leader as he lies in state in the Capitol.

Page 55—Mourners assemble at the Capitol Sunday afternoon.

Page 56, top—Through the night they came to mourn.

Page 56, bottom—Mourners file past the bier in the Capitol Rotunda.

Page 57—Pope Paul VI offers Requiem Mass at St. Peter's basilica in Rome.

Page 58—Lee Harvey Oswald is accosted by Jack Ruby (copyright The Dallas Morning News, photo by Jack Beers).

Page 59—Lee Harvey Oswald grimaces as he is shot by Jack Ruby (copyright The Dallas Times-Herald, photo by Robert Jackson).

Page 60—Mrs. Kennedy and Sen. Edward Kennedy kneel at the bier in the Capitol Rotunda.

Pages 61-62—The coffin is borne from the Capitol.

Page 64—Mourners at the Capitol.

Page 65—The cortege departs from the Capitol.

Page 66—The riderless horse, boots reversed in the stirrups, a symbol of the fallen hero.

Page 67—The President's widow and his brothers arrive for the funeral Mass at St. Matthew's Cathedral. President and Mrs. Johnson are in the background.

Pages 68-69, top—Heads of state and foreign dignitaries leave the White House in the funeral march to St. Matthew's.

Page 69, bottom—The cortege leaves the White House enroute to St. Matthew's Cathedral.

Page 70—Richard Cardinal Cushing precedes the coffin into St. Matthew's Cathedral.

Page 70, bottom—Richard Cardinal Cushing consoles Mrs. Kennedy at St. Matthew's.

Page 71—The nation's military leaders in the funeral procession.

Page 72—Mrs. Kennedy and her children, John, Jr., and Caroline.

Page 73—Mrs. Kennedy and her children arrive at St. Matthew's.

Page 74, top—The coffin rests before the main altar during the Requiem Mass.

Page 74, bottom—John F. Kennedy, Jr. in the center aisle at St. Matthew's Cathedral.

Page 75, top—Mrs. Kennedy and her children, and the President's mother, leave St. Matthew's Cathedral.

Page 75, bottom—Former Presidents Harry S. Truman and Dwight D. Eisenhower, and Mrs. Eisenhower, leave St. Matthew's Cathedral.

Page 76—Mrs. Joseph P. Kennedy, the President's mother and Robert Fitzgerald, the President's cousin, arrive at St. Matthew's.

Page 77—The coffin is borne from St. Matthew's Cathedral.

Page 78—President Kennedy's famed rocking chairs awaiting removal from the White House

Page 79—Mrs. Kennedy at the steps of St. Matthew's Cathedral

Page 80—John F. Kennedy, Jr. salutes his father.

Page 81—President Charles de Gaulle of France, Chancellor Ludwig Erhard of West Germany (in foreground with overcoat), and Emperor Haile Selassie of Ethiopia

Page 82—Former Presidents Eisenhower and Truman depart from St Matthew's Cathedral.

Page 83—The cortege as viewed from Arlington Cemetery.

Page 84, top—Viewed from the Lincoln Memorial, the procession moves toward Arlington National Cemetery across Memorial Bridge.

Pages 84-85, bottom — The horse-drawn caisson proceeds through Arlington National Cemetery

Pages 86-87—The brother, mother and widow of the President arrive as the coffin is placed at the grave.

Page 88—Mourners at Arlington.

Page 89—The honor guard places the coffin at the grave

Page 90—Mrs. Kennedy holds the flag which covered the President's coffin.

Page 91—The eternal flame.

Page 92—The President's mother, his brother, the Attorney General, and Mrs. Kennedy, at the burial.

Page 93—President Charles de Gaulle of France—among other dignitaries—salutes as President Kennedy is laid to rest.

Page 94, left—The coffin is lowered as officer salutes.

Page 94, right—Mourner kneels as the President is laid to rest.

Page 95—Nuns utter a prayer at the grave.

Page 96—The honor guard stands vigil at the President's grave at dawn Tuesday.

Page 97—Mrs. Kennedy visits her husband's grave on Tuesday.

Page 98—President Lyndon B. Johnson addresses a joint session of Congress.

CPSIA information can be obtained
at www.ICGtesting.com
Printed in the USA
BVHW022255260123
657282BV00004B/20